T0146587

The Way

The Truth

and

The Life

Jesus saith unto him, I am the way, the truth, and the life; no man cometh unto the Father, but by me."

Mickey R. Mullen

Mickey R. Mullen

THE WAY

THE TRUTH

AND

THE LIFE

Mickey R. Mullen

National Library of Canada Cataloguing in Publication Data

Mullen, Mickey Ray, 1937-
  The way the truth and the life

  Includes bibliographical references.
  ISBN 1-55212-774-5

  1. Mullen, Mickey Ray, 1937- 2. Christian biography.
I. Title.
BR1725.M63A3 2001   248.4   C2001-910782-X

TRAFFORD

This book was published *on-demand* **in cooperation with Trafford Publishing.**
On-demand publishing is a unique process and service of making a book available for retail sale to the public taking advantage of on-demand manufacturing and Internet marketing.
On-demand publishing includes promotions, retail sales, manufacturing, order fulfilment, accounting and collecting royalties on behalf of the author.

Suite 6E, 2333 Government St., Victoria, B.C. V8T 4P4, CANADA

Phone	250-383-6864	Toll-free	1-888-232-4444 (Canada & US)
Fax	250-383-6804	E-mail	sales@trafford.com
Web site	www.trafford.com	TRAFFORD PUBLISHING IS A DIVISION OF TRAFFORD HOLDINGS LTD.
Trafford Catalogue #01-0174		www.trafford.com/robots/01-0174.html

10   9   8   7   6

TABLE OF CONTENTS

INTRODUCTION

From that time many of his disciples went back, and walked no more with him. Then said Jesus unto the twelve, Will ye also go away? Then Simon Peter answered him, Lord, to whom shall we go? Thou hast the words of eternal life. St John 6 v 66-68

Jesus saith unto them, Have ye understood all these things? They say unto him, Yea, Lord. Then said he unto them, Therefore every scribe (scholar) *which is instructed unto the kingdom of heaven is like unto a man that is a householder, which bringeth forth out of his treasure things new and old.* (After conversion and when living as a sinner.) St Matthew 13 v 51 & 52

Now his parents went to Jerusalem every year at the feast of the Passover, and when he was twelve years old, they went up to Jerusalem; after the custom of the feast. And when they had filled the days, as they returned, the child Jesus tarried behind in Jerusalem; and Joseph and his mother knew not of it. But they, supposing him to have been in the company, went a day's journey; and they sought him among their kinsfolk and acquaintance. And when they found him not, they turned back again to Jerusalem, seeking him. And it came to pass, that after three days they found him in the temple, sitting in the midst of the doctors, both hearing them, and asking them questions. and all that heard him were astonished at his understanding and answers. And when they saw him they were amazed: and his mother said unto him, Son, why hast thou thus dealt with us? Behold, thy father and I have sought thee sorrowing. And he said unto

them, How is it that ye sought me? Wist ye not that I must be about my Father's business? And they understood not the saying which he spake unto them. And he went down with them, and came to Nazareth, and was subject unto them: but his mother kept all these saying in her heart. And Jesus increased in wisdom and stature, and in favor with God and man.
St Luke 2 v 41 - 52

My Life
Part 1

I was born on September 20, 1937, in Laramie, Wyoming, descended from Irish ancestors, as well as the Cherokee Indians who had marched on the "Trail of Tears." The Cherokees were forced to march from the Carolinas, on the East Coast, to Oklahoma.

My Dad, Mike, got his first good job working on the railroad. Living in a homemade trailer built on a truck frame, it was about 16 feet long, with a wood or coal stove for heat and cooking. With one brother, Paul, seven years older, and a sister, Sis (Margarita), five years older, there was very little room to move around. Anyone that wants to go back to the "good old days" doesn't know what they're talking about. Paul said that he lived in the trailer four years. Sis must have lived in it for two years. You have heard of trailer trash—well, we lived in a trashy trailer.

The family told me that before they arrived in Laramie, they had gone to Kansas "to follow the harvest." Families used to work in the wheat fields when the wheat was ready to harvest. I was told that the grasshoppers liked the linseed oil that Dad put on the canvas, "the siding," and ate holes in it.

With not much of a car, Dad came upon this hill that was too steep for the car to pull the trailer up. Dad found a brick and told Paul that when he popped the clutch, to move the brick up behind the wheel—at least once Paul got his fingers pinched between the brick and the tire.

After the Kansas escapade, my family went to Laramie. It was one of Paul's jobs to pull his wagon along the railroad track and put coal in it that had "accidentally" fallen off the train."

When the time came for me to be born, Mom went to a house in the stock yards where the midwife lived. The morning I was born, Dad came in shortly afterward and found me laying on a bed with no blanket over me. Outside a winter snow storm was raging. I got an ear infection, and the doctor lanced it. It was a family joke, since I had freckles, to say that "the cow blew bran in my face" when I was born in the stock yards.

With a job and credit at the lumber yard, Dad bought a lot and started building a house, with me placed in a corner, when I wasn't breast feeding. Dad, as soon as he could, got the basement ready, put a floor on it and it served as the roof when we moved in. Then he finished the rest of the house. After living in the trailer it was a move up. Paul told me he helped dig the basement by hand. If I was to see that house today, the basement would be what I would be interested in. If there was concrete walls and floor it would surprise me. Can you imagine the noise that I had to endure as a new born baby?

The house in Laramie Dad built. Paul and Matthew on stoop, 1997.

Newsweek had a "special 2000 edition" about child development from birth to three years old; it was devoted to the critical age of a child. It gave me a good insight of why I am like I am. In the article it says trusting develops the first three months of life (if he cries he gets picked up). I doubt if this occurred as much as it should have. Mom had a bad leg from polio and she had to help Dad as much as she could. Even when I was in the womb her walk was not steady. Things like "a lovely sweet-potato purée, accompanied by a gentle back rub," was not in the cards. "When a baby smells his mother's skin, the olfactory signal reaching the brain triggers the formation of neuronal links between it and the brain's memory and emotion centers. As a result, the baby remembers Mom's smell and associates it with pleasant events," the article reads. Mom must have smelled like fresh concrete and tar.

The article continues. "Children who haven't had the benefit of nurturing adults early on have trouble even forming friendships, let alone negotiating the inevitable ups and downs of these relationships. As children's behavior becomes more complex in the second year of life, they learn from their caregivers' facial expressions, tone of voice, gestures and words, what kinds of behavior lead to approval or disapproval," it reads. Yeah, like when Dad tore into Paul when he had a migraine headache. Not being able to form friendships has plagued me all my life.

"The give-and-take between children and caregivers creates patterns of behavior," the article continues. They must be talking about Dad giving and us taking. When we had company I would hide behind Mom's dress, no matter what she was doing, she had to wear one, because of the church rules.

I had most of the "bad habits" like sucking my thumb—pacifiers were not invented yet. Biting my fingernails—a habit that I have never been able to break. When I started walking, Rex (Paul's Dog) and I tried to run away from home. By then, though, Rex had found out all about Dad's foot.

Playing on the floor one day when I was four years old, I saw my parents having sex on the couch. The next day I was caught playing with a neighbor boy's penis and was brought in the house by Mom. Two hours later when Dad came home from work, he went into a rage and went out to the nearest tree and got several switches. He came at me in two separate volleys, the second was worse than the first.

To this day I have scars from my knees to my waist—it was the only beating that I ever received. In the first or second grade the teacher spanked a pupil with switches that she made him go outside and get. After that happened I thought it was normal, for sure.

Left to right: Mickey, Sis, Paul, and dog Rex in Laramie, Wyoming, 1942.

It is my understanding that the school—Hickory Grove—is still there today.

The students at Hickory Grove School in Seneca, Missouri in 1943. Mickey is in first grade; Mickey is second child from left in the second row; Sis is the second child from right, fourth row.

All my self-esteem was totally lost. Paul had migraine headaches and Dad told me later in life, the reason he spanked him so much was he thought Paul was trying to get out of work. Sis received a few but not too many. He never hit Mom but often threatened to. His favorite way to blow off steam was to slam doors—it didn't matter if they were on the car or in the house. Showing God that he never spared the rod, Dad was called to preach. *He that spareth his rod hateth his son: but he that loveth him chasteneth him betimes.* Proverbs 13 v 24

My granddad died in 1930 from a loss of blood. The doctor put leaches on him to "bleed" him and he left them on his body too long, a common practice at that time. Paul came down with appendicitis before we left Laramie and it burst. The doctor inserted a tube that drained the poison out that he left in for several days.

After quitting his job on the railroad, that was a deferment in World War II, Dad bought a farm in Seneca, Missouri. The farm was more hill and rocks then anything else, but we did have a space for a garden in the spring. It was getting through the first winter that was tough. Beans and cornbread was about all we had to eat. Paul shot rabbits and squirrels. In addition, we'd eat bull frog legs and wild honey—whatever we could find—for a change of diet.

Mickey with a cat on the Missouri farm.

I have a videotape of Dad telling us that we ate the same bran that he fed the horses. Leftover corn bread, if there was any, I ate for breakfast with sugar and milk. Our first garden in the spring the weeds was performing better than anything else, so Dad was going to show Mom, "a thing or two." He hitched up one of the smarter horses to the plow, and proceeded to plow under the weeds. I believe most people would use a hoe, delicately, around each plant. It was the last time he hoed the weeds with the plow.

Dad on the farm with the team—Dick and Duke.

We had family "get togethers" once in a while. At these events it was explained to me that girls was made of sugar and spice and everything nice. You can imagine what boys was made of.

When we went to town once a week, at the movie theater I noticed that on the billboards was a picture of Shirley Temple that looked like she was my age. It left little doubt that I had gotten on the wrong train. Dad didn't believe in going to movies so it was years before I went.

Usually on Saturday we took Mom's eggs to town and sold them to get supplies. It was a time to spend our allowance—25 or 50 cents, and Paul got a dollar. I usually ended up with the biggest share, even with my 25 cent nest egg. I would go up to each one at a time and tell them that if they would give me a nickel to go with my nickel I could buy a big bag of candy. No wonder business has been my forte, along with a dozen other occupations over the years (any of which I could have made a living at). If there was an Aunt Jemima, I saw her in Seneca at a grocery store; she was making pancakes for the customers. She was the first black person I ever saw. Dad noticed my wide-eyed amazement and took me down to a bridge near by. There was a rope hanging from a tree limb that looked like it had been there awhile. He said Aunt Jemima had to be out of town by sun down—the last one that stayed after sun down was hung with that rope. If the truth was known, at one time that rope probably had a tire tied to it and the kids swung out over the water and dropped in.

We had a radio that worked with a car battery. The only time we had permission to bring it in the house was when Joe Louis had a title match. Paul would bring it in, when the coast was clear we would listen to Amos and Andy, Intersanktum, the Squeaking Door, Green Hornet, Tonto, Little Red Rider, and those other old wonderful radio shows.

We used a Sears catalog for toilet paper—back then all we had was an old outhouse. The best time to "go" was after it rained when the paper was moist and soft. One day I was doing my daily in the outhouse when I couldn't seem to get rid of the thing hanging out my rectum. Sis heard me yelling and came over to see what the problem was. I showed her and she ran to the house to get help. It was the only time that I saw a doctor until after my parents' divorce. It was a worm about eight inches long.

When we ran out of sugar or couldn't afford it, we use honey, sorghum, or molasses instead. During the World War II you needed a coupon to buy items like sugar and gas for the car, but because we lived on a farm we got extra gas coupons. With our money, we never ran out of coupons for gas.

Whenever Dad would butcher a hog or calf all the fat was heated to make lard and lye was added to make soap to wash the clothes on a wash board by hand and bathe. Our water on both farms was taken from a well outside. Every Saturday night we heated water on a wood cook stove and took a bath in a galvanized tub about three feet in diameter. I took my bath first with the only clean water of the night (the smallest person first). It was real dirty after that. As each one of the rest of the family took a bath, hot water was added to the tub.

Mom heated heavy irons on the cook stove for ironing the clothes. For years, in every school, when they examined me they sent a note home that I needed my tonsils removed. I suffered for years with them. After the eventual divorce when I was 13 years old Mom finally had that done, they were close to exploding. She also had my rotten teeth filled. Today I still have enough to eat with after two gingivitis operations. With no indoor plumbing until I was 12, it's a miracle I had any teeth at all. All the credit goes to Mom. If every person had a mother like her, the world would be a better place.

My mother, Ida.

Sometime when Dad and Mom were talking, as far back as I can remember, they said they were going to have it done. The problem was they always looked in my direction. I didn't know if I wanted it done—"it" didn't sound good to me. Finally after years of torment they quit talking about it, and I learned that "it" was circumcision. It took me years to figure it out. Remember, I was born in a house—not a hospital. Paul was circumcised when he was 10 or 11 years old, that would make me three or four. It is interesting to me that they didn't have me circumcised at the same time. Biblically it is not necessary for this dispensation.

Most of the time because of my age I played outside. Mom couldn't get my neck clean for church and told Dad. He put his knee in my chest on the floor and proceeded to wash my neck. It damaged my vocal cords.
Dad said it was sacrilegious to pray if you're not saved. I believe he was right. When I was asked to pray, dismissing Sunday school, I never said a word. If the teacher ever said anything to Dad, I'm unaware of it. The children never prayed at home at bed time or any other time.

Convert according to the dictionary means to change, transform. In the concordance and the dictionary there is the word, "turn again." If one is "raised up in the way they should go" why did Jesus die on the Cross? If, as a child when they start talking, you send them to bed and tell them to say their prayers, I would be the first one to say how cute it is. The only problem we have is, where is a scripture for cute? Saying grace at the dinner table is another cute thing to do. So the question is, is it turn or change - transform? You see I believe it is transform. Children then become grown-up with this false sense of security and become divinity experts or theologians, which is a crucial criterion to be excepted as a leader in some if not most churches.

Therefore speak I to them in parables: because they seeing see not; and hearing they hear not, neither do they understand. And in them is fulfilled the prophecy of Isaiah, which saith, By hearing ye shall hear, and shall not understand; and seeing ye shall see, and shall not perceive: for this people's heart is waxed gross, and their ears are dull of hearing, and their eyes they have closed; Lest at any time they SHOULD see with their eyes, and hear with your ears, and SHOULD understand with their HEART, and SHOULD be CONVERTED, and I SHOULD heal them. But blessed are your eyes, for they see: and your ears, for they hear. St Matthew 13 v 13-16

The first church Dad thought Paul "acted up," and took him outside and spanked him. Paul told Dad that he would never go to church again, and never did during that era. When we got to Seneca, Dad's relatives were in the area, so I was told at a "get together." I went outside and got a stick and came back into the house and poked a newborn baby's eye out. I can vaguely remember doing such a thing. You have to remember that this was not too long after the beating.

Dad got another call, this time from the Army (after all World War II was still in progress). He hot footed it to Kansas City and got back on the railroad. He told me he ran into a previous boss that he had in Laramie. Paul was 12 when he became, "the farmer," and Mom, with only one good leg because of polio worked like a dog. I wish I could say that in another way.

It was always her job to get up in a cold house in the morning and get the fire started for heat. At night we lined up and took a hot brick covered with newspapers to bed with us. My parents took the hot water bottle to bed with them. Sis did as much as she could and I was five years old, too young for the first grade, "but took it all in."

Our next door neighbor was a deacon in a Baptist church and was a big help, not only with teaching Paul how to farm, but he would also visit with Mom in the bed room when everybody else was in school.

There was a lot of men "off to the war." I never knew why the kindly neighbor wasn't storming a beach head somewhere. He had a highly spirited horse that would make Trigger look like a Shetland pony.

One time when Mom was in the kitchen I asked her if she ever read the Bible? When she came down with a "women sickness," Dad took her to Kansas City for the "cure."

Ever so often Dad would come back to the farm and then drive back to his job. On one trip he said that two motorcycles were in his lane of traffic and when he got out of their way he went off the road. The Model A Ford that was a convertible rolled over and let him out. It landed on its wheels with the Bible still on the seat. Dad said he preached a sermon then and there to those who stopped.

After the sermon he got back in the car and drove to Kansas City. He went down to a lumber yard and bought a house window. He somehow installed it for a windshield, used plexiglas for the rest of the windows and covered it all with canvas. This Ford was one of our better cars, it replaced a Model A that we had to start with a crank.

Both of the Model As had a rumble seat in the back, where the kids sat most of the time. Whenever Dad was ready to go he would grab me by one arm and put me up in the seat. I must have been five, six, seven, and possibly eight years old when he did this. I always tried to get up in the rumble seat before this occurred but sometimes it was difficult to get the timing right.

The second farm house our family lived in. Dad and Mickey on Paul's scooter.

Dad bought 40 acres of timber, about a mile away, and he was going to "clear the land" to grow strawberries. Dick (the horse) was the best horse in the state, but it turned out to be an impossible task with the equipment that we possessed, or the tenacity on Dad's part. One day I went with Dad and left to play in the woods. When I got lost, Dad went back to the farm without me at quitting time. As the story goes, when he walked in the

22

house his brother was there and Mom asked Dad "where is Mickey?" Dad said that the hogs ate him, that's when the pot of beans went flying through the air. Uncle Leroy said, "I think I'll go back home now."

Dad added a kitchen on to the back of the house and Paul was cleaning his 22 rifle when Mom decided to get up from the chair to fix supper. That's when the gun went off and went through the back of the chair. Paul found a huge turtle that was two to three feet in diameter; it was probably 100 years old, and for some reason known only to God and our neighbor next door, he used a team of horses and wagon to make mush of it on the road. I guess it never was introduced to man before.

At the farm in Miami there was a windmill at the back of the house connected to a generator that made electricity. A thunder storm came up, close to a tornado in velocity, and Dad was playing one of his favorite games with me on the floor. He had my head in his crotch throwing my body side to side. Sis was trying to get in the house at the back door but the rain had swollen it and it wouldn't open. She ran toward the front door and the windmill going at supersonic speed came crashing down behind her. That was the end of the electric power.

One time Mom sent me to school with a boiled egg for lunch, it was common practice to break the shell on each other's head. Unfortunately, Mom had forgotten something—my egg was fresh and I can still see the yellow running down the other kid's face.

Paul had gotten a Model A from someplace and took the body off of it. About all that was left was the motor front seat and steering wheel. After he took it for a test drive he drove up to me and ask me if I wanted to go for a ride? I hopped in and put my bare foot down on the "hot exhaust pipe," that felt good, just what I needed!

When World War II ended, Dad quit his job on the railroad again and he bought another farm near Miami, Oklahoma. He couldn't stand prosperity. He gave my dog Trixie to the farmer that helped us out (in more ways then

23

one). I never could understand it because we moved from one farm to another. If I remember right he was the one that gave me the dog in the first place. It was a rat terrier that had plenty to do on the farm. A cat that stayed out in the barn would disappear up to three weeks and when it showed up would have a rabbit in its mouth, which Dad would put in the garbage can. It would hang around a month and then go missing again.

I had to take the third grade twice because we moved in the middle of the school year. The second farm had more land for farming, if you could call it that. Dad (having been ordained) after returning from Kansas City was accepted at another church.

One Wednesday night, Dad went to church by himself. When he arrived, he got out of the car there was a half frozen chicken stuck to the top. He pulled it lose and put it inside of the car. Mom put it in the oven the next day. We had a dinner at one of Dad's brothers house and had some chicken left over. His wife threw it out. When Raymond came home from work, he said that all he wanted was amustard sandwich, any way. We were not allowed to eat between meals.

One of Dad's churches, taken sometime in 1990.

After remodeling the church, he was moving their new piano in a truck when it tipped over, sending its parts scattering all over the road. He was ready to leave anyway.

There was no such thing as not being hungry when it was ready. After the evening meal it was safe to indulge in a pickle and mustard sandwich. It was just like going to a hamburger joint. Bread, butter, and sugar was a delicacy. Mom always ate the back of a chicken; the neck was my piece. Paul and Sis couldn't remember eating chicken feet but I sure did. It is common in some of the other countries. You have to take the scales off, sort of like lobster, but a little different.

When I went to college, the teacher couldn't believe that I was never in a food fight. The plate where the fried chicken had been I took a slice of bread and sopped up the plate after the meal. Dad would cure a ham either with salt or sugar and hang it up in the barn, underestimating the tenacious-ness of a starving cat. More then once the ham would be on the ground in the morning. It wasn't beneath us to eat the seed potatoes that were meant for the garden. I read one time that if you run out of options, take a sack of potatoes with you, then you can either eat them or plant them. Forget the gold under the bed.

In the winter time Paul said he cut blocks of ice on a pond and put them in a cellar covered up with straw for the ice box. When we ran out they bought a block of ice on Saturday, if that disappeared we were out until the next Saturday. We never drank very much pop, but on the Fourth of July we would get pop and go on a picnic, the main course would be fried chicken. There was no way we could have a picnic without watermelon and they always bought me a buffalo. Another family joke — it was canta-loupe.

It was one of my quirks to have motion sickness in a car. Dad, Mom, and I in the front seat of a Model A Ford was going to church. I told Dad that he better stop, he kept going. It wasn't long before I lunged across Mom to the open window. Dad knew that I needed help then, he turned the wheel in the opposite direction, and slammed on the brakes. It slammed my head into the top of the door, with my body thrown against the dash. Do you want to feel my knot? I got sick all over Mom's dress, made with three flour sacks. At that time flour came in sacks with a design on them and most of the bread was homemade, so it never took long to get enough for a dress. A bird could fly through Mom's panties hanging on the clothes line without ducking.

I must have been about seven years old when one Sunday morning at church, a family we had never seen before was there. It was always better if we got invited for dinner after the service because of the distance back to the farm. This new family invited us for dinner. It was not long after we got there that the man started pinching my penis with his fingers, right in front of Dad and Mom. He did it so often that when dinner was ready, Mom fixed me a plate and I ate out in the barn. When we were driving away, with our bellies full, Dad said "maybe we should have left or said something to him."

If there was anyone that heard every one of Dad's sermons it was me. I was too young to resist. If he ever got more tithes then $7 a week I wouldn't know when it was. He couldn't remember going to school. In town one time Mom stopped at the Salvation Army and bought me a pair of shoes (10 cents). When we were walking up to Dad, I was all excited, I said, "new shoes, Daddy, new shoes." The only problem was I could only wear them to town, church, and school.

Sis was chopping wood one time with a double-bitted ax, it never went through the short log so I pushed my left foot down on the opposite end and nearly got my two toes cut off. Kerosene was what she put on my foot until we went to town and bought peroxide. Mom wanted to take me to a doctor but Dad couldn't afford it.

Mom told Sis to go out and cut the head off a chicken for supper. She put the head on the chopping block, it moved and she only cut half the head off. The chicken took off running. We had a hard time catching it. Dad had his own way of, "doing a chicken." He showed me how to do it several times. He would put the chicken's head in his hand and twist its head off. When that didn't work he put his shoe on its head on the ground, and pulled its head off.

All the farming was done with "abused" horses. To get the hair off of a hog you need a little hot water and a knife. Dad decided to pull a freshly killed hog, with a rope through a pulley in a tree, above a 55 gallon barrel filled with the " right amount of water." A fire was under the barrel. With the horse tied to the end of the rope he said, "giddy up" and the horse went back to the barn. The hog went up to the pulley, but the rope broke and the hog fell into the hot boiling water. Dad went through this twice using a different horse the second time.

With not enough money coming in from his preaching, Dad bought a hay bailer that required one horse as the energy source. It was my job to walk behind the horse with it tied to a pole. It ran the bailer, a plunger mechanism pushed the hay inside the hopper down, when the hay was placed in it. Two people, usually Mom and Sis, tied the bails with twine. First you had to cut the weeds with a little hay in it, and rake it over to the bailer, using the other two horses. Then using a pitch fork, placing the weeds in the hopper. Keeping the horse walking around the circle was my job. Walking on the weed stubs was the bad part, with no shoes. Dad was so impressed with his crew he hired us out to the neighbors.

One of the neighbors was not too far away so Dad received a revelation, Instead of taking Mohammed to the mountain, he would bring the mountain to Mohammed. He piled the wagon as high as he could with hay, with me sitting on top of it. Mom arrived just in time and told Dad to get me off the top. When he drove the wagon on to the road it tilted a little and it turned over, with the top of the hay hitting a barbed wire fence. The horses panicked and drug the wagon on its side a couple miles. I can't remember if we ever replaced it or not.

Half the time our milk tasted like weeds. Dad seemed to watch for the time when the horse and I had trampled the weeds and hay down and my feet wasn't hurting. He even committed about it, it was at this time he would move the bailer to a different location where the pain would start all over again. The nerve endings are connected to the bottom of your feet, or so

I've read. My nerves were damaged.

For a while Dad had a "milk route" in Miami but his customers weren't used to the weed taste. One time Paul was trying to push the mixture down into the hopper with his leg when it went in too deep. I told the horse to "woe" and it did. Paul was removing an object from the sickle that cut the hay, the horse moved and the blade moved, he thought he cut his finger off, he grabbed a rag and wrapped his hand in it. With blood all over the place, Dad took off flying down the road in our trusty Model A and got him to the doctor. The doctor showed Dad his cut and they drove back to the farm. Dad and Paul should have gotten together this once about what they were going to do. When Paul finished his job he was galloping Prince (a horse) back to the barn. It was the same day that Dad put a barbed wire fence across the usual path, when Prince saw it he shied, and Paul went off on his head. It knocked him out for a few minutes. Dad was smoothing a freshly plowed field with about a 16-foot board with spikes protruding out of the bottom. The job only required one horse and chain attached to the center of the board where he stood. I came along and said "Dad could I have a ride?" He said to hop on. So I hopped on the end of it and the spikes dug into the dirt and the board stopped momentarily and then it took off—luckily I fell behind the board and not in front of it.

Paul graduated from high school wearing Uncle Leroy's suit coat and Dad's pants. Finally Dad and Paul got in a wrestling match and he told Paul the farm was not big enough for two men. Paul went to Bettendorf, Iowa, and worked in construction until he decided to join the Air Force. He bought a 1947 Chusman scooter, so Dad went and got it and brought it back to the farm. I never knew why he never resold it.

When he came home after the Korean War it was a wreck, because Dad, Sis, and I started riding it when I was nine years old. You learn responsibility early when riding on the highway when one wrong move could be a death sentence. At that time I didn't need a drivers license.

Paul with our Dad.

Paul spent the next 20 years in the Air Force, retired, and then went to college, eventually receiving a doctorate. He taught in a university for several years until retiring permanently.

With Paul gone, Mom knew she had a problem getting the work done. So she talked Dad into quitting preaching and convinced him to become a carpenter, which he did. World War II was over, and the world never came to an end, as some that read the Bible thought. He gave most everything away.

When we were going to buy the trailer in Tulsa, I came down with pink eye. My eyes were pink and matted together, especially in the morning. I had to get them open with a cloth saturated with warm water. Dad had prearranged to bring a utility trailer overflowing with our stuff from the farm and left it to be auctioned off. We went on to buy a Spartan, 8-by-29-foot trailer in Tulsa, Oklahoma.

The first trailer. Sis is on Paul's scooter. Mickey with stray dog.

On the way back to the farm, Dad stopped to shovel the money in the car, like you do when you go to Las Vegas, Nevada. It had rained that day and the auctioneer told Dad, " there wasn't any money." So everything was left there anyway. That has left a bitter taste in my mouth ever since with auctions. Dad was bitter to his death because of Mom wanting him to stop preaching.

This was a side of Dad that Paul never saw: Dad took Rex out in a field and shot him while we were in school. (The poor dog never got a square meal in his life.) Dad waited a week until Sis and I had our last day in school, and left without our grades. It was the first time that Dad ever waited. Our first stop was Davenport, Iowa, where Mom's sister lived. My aunt's live-in, Ray Keith, was a Union carpenter with black and blue fingers.

The next several years were hell on earth. We moved up to three times a school year. Dad's favorite place to park the trailer was in the sun, trying to tell Mom something I guess. Dad always said children were to be seen and not heard. In school when we went north every child in my class would turn around to stare when the teacher called on me, because of my southern accent. At the end of the school year the teacher would usually ask me, "who are you?"

Sis with the Spartan trailer.

I always played an angel in Christmas plays. In the trailer park Sis and her girl friend was playing in a tent. I opened the flap that was the door and Sis hit me square in the nose with the palm of her hand; if she used her fist maybe it wouldn't have hurt as much. When we came home from school and saw the car hitched up to the trailer we knew Dad had gotten laid off or fired. He put the Chusman scooter in the front room of the trailer, with the fuel oil barrel. Never, did I know of, did he ask the carpenter business agent for another job in the same town where we were at the time.

Dad got a union carpenter card when he showed the business agent a picture of the house he built in Laramie, Wyoming. When we arrived in Galena, Illinois, with no brakes, coming down the hill into town, it is beyond me how he did it. There is a God. In the vicinity of the steering column would be two wires that operated the electric brakes on the trailer. Maybe he couldn't get his wires together.

Sis quit school in the 10th grade and got married to Merlyn, probably the nicest person that I have ever met, and raised a fine family in Cuba City, Wisconsin, that left all the couch for me to sleep on, and I'm not talking about one with a bed inside of it. When I go visit them, it is fun to pal around with Karla, one of their daughters. Sis gave birth to five children.

Sis and Merlyn on their wedding day, 1950.

When we left Galena, Dad had two towns he could go to: one of them was Sioux City, Iowa, and the other Pierre, South Dakota. When we got to Sioux City a car full of young adults was harassing us. Dad's teeth had already been knocked out with brass knuckles when he was about 21 years old, "both sets." We went on to Pierre. In 1998, I was driving through Sioux City and on the interstate I kept looking for a sign that said gas. It was the second time I went through that town without stopping.

When we got to Rapid City, South Dakota, Dad was working at the Air Force base. It was here that we totally quit going to church. In Sunday school Dad never agreed with the teacher about something and we left right after Sunday school, which was unusual. Backing up to get out of the parking lot, he ran into a light pole.

Mom read in a newspaper that one of the motels needed someone to run it, and they had a space for a trailer. It was the third time Mom worked, the other two times was in Pierre and Sioux Falls in commercial laundries. They moved the trailer to the motel.

In about a year Mom read that a man wanted to sell a half-finished house, and they bought it. It was made out of homemade concrete blocks. Because Dad was working, I made almost all the blocks. To this day, I can remember the mixture that I used: one part cement, two parts sand, and three gravel. We used a small mixer with an electric motor. To lay the blocks and stucco the inside walls, we mixed the mud by hand in a homemade box.

The block house in Rapid City Mickey made the blocks for; Dad is on the roof.

Mickey R. Mullen

The house we made withstood the 1972 flood, although it was only two blocks from the Rapid City creek. I was 12 years old and did it after school. Cleaning the forms and putting them together one day, and filling them the next. The man that sold us the house let us use the forms he designed and when we got the blocks made he laid them. Part of the deal, if we bought the property.

After the walls were up Dad asked Ray Keith to come and help him put the roof on, which he did. After I finished making the blocks, Dad had a man and a back hoe dig the sewer line, but he could only dig it to the wall, so I had to dig it the rest of the way to the middle of the house.

It was about Christmas and Dad said, "well Mick, let's go down to the hardware store and I'll buy you a new bike." Mom came with us in the pickup truck. I picked out a Swain bike, the first new bike I ever had. I said, "Dad, I'll ride it home." He said, "no, put it out behind the truck." Parking it behind the truck, I got in the cab with Mom. When Dad was ready to go he went, so I had already learned to get in the truck if I knew he was coming. After he paid for it, he came out got in the truck and backed over the bike. I don't remember him ever taking anything back in his life. Perhaps he could have done something if he went in and talked to the staff of the store. He got out and threw the bike in the back of the truck and we went home.

I believe Mom had other things on her mind after the house was built, because the next year my parents were divorced, and she paid Dad for half the house, working at the Duck Inn Cafe, washing dishes for $24 a week. She received no child support. Dad was my legal guardian—if you could find him. It was fun filling out the paper work in school. I lived with Mom, who became an excellent cook at the Cafe. When the divorce was final, Mom asked Dad to do one thing in the house. A stud had bowed in the kitchen and she asked him if he would make a cabinet in the wall to put a set of china that Paul had sent her from Japan during the Korea War.

Mom and Dad next to the block house; the second trailer is in the background.

Dad was going to Casper, Wyoming, and showed up the next morning. He always wanted someone around when he worked and he worked on that cabinet and cried all day. It was the worst day of my life, and I have had some miserable days. Dad would tell anyone that wanted to know, that after the divorce he started drinking and was drunk a good share of the time for the next 30 years. The truth is, he was riding back and forth to the job and the men would stop at a bar after work and have a beer. Dad went from pop to beer in a short time, but I never saw him drunk until after the divorce.

In school my grades were mostly average before the divorce. After the divorce it was real strange going to the same school all year. In 13 years of school, I skipped school one day in the 12th grade, with very few sick days. One morning I told Mom that I hated to go to school 13 years with out skipping school, so I put the 22 rifle in the trunk to go rabbit hunting. Driving out of town, when I got about three miles I saw some lights flashing behind me. I was wondering how the police found out about me skipping school. They drove up behind me, and told me to open my trunk and they found the rifle. One of my neighbor's saw me putting a rifle in the trunk. The night before two men in the jail had escaped. Satisfied I wasn't taking the gun to them they let me go.

Getting a job when I was 14 at a Green House until they ask me if I could drive a car. After working there a year, I had to say no. The first drink I had was at their Christmas party: whiskey and eggnog. Dad had left the Chusman scooter with me and one day going home from the Green House a car came around a corner and turned left right in front of me. It took all the skin off my left hand. I laid the scooter down on the gravel and set on top of it until it stopped moving. That was the only wreck that I ever had with it. The scooter never did run right after that.

Trailer #2. The "green" trailer Dad lived in for about thirty years.

In 1957 I had my one and only car wreck ($150 damage, when the police were called). Groceries were a problem without a car but I could take some home on the scooter before, but now we had a problem. Dad just happened to come back to work at the Air Force base, and he was visiting one day. I asked if I could drive him to his trailer. I backed out of Mom's drive way and drove his shift type truck the three blocks.Deer hunting season was open, so I asked Dad if he would drive me toward Mount Rushmore and let me out of the truck to hunt deer. I told him when I was ready to come home, I would call Mom and her boyfriend would come get me. He said okay. Getting a license, the great white hunter was ready. Paul had brought a Korean gun home with him, with armor piercing shells that was illegal.

Dad took me about 20 miles up into the Black Hills and let me out. I must have been 14 years old at the time. Walking about a mile in the trees I was setting on a log eating a sandwich. A doe came walking through the woods. Taking careful aim, I fired the gun, and the doe ran a half block and fell down. I couldn't believe it.

The next chore was getting it to the road and calling Mom. Her boy friend and Mom showed up and he put the deer in the trunk of the car and closed the lid. They took it to have it cut up and wrapped, about a half hour we got a call. The meat was spoiled. I was suppose to have cut the throat of the deer to bleed it and remove the inside parts (gut it).

Behind Mom's house was a produce company and it had snowed during the night. On the way to school with a snowball in my hand I heard a familiar truck coming. So I let it fly and I wish the driver had his side window rolled up. I found a new route to school. At one o'clock when I got to work a truck was backed up to the back door that looked familiar, the driver was showing my boss his knot on the side of his head.

With money that I had saved, I bought a 1940 Chevrolet when I was 15 years old. Then I got a job at the Sooper Dooper Market for $125 a mouth, working 60 hours a week, and started smoking. Going to work one day I was speeding and passed a cop, going in the opposite direction. I don't know what got in me. I pushed down on the gas when I saw him turning around. Going around a curve I headed for a gas station that I traded at every day, the grease rack was empty so I pulled in. The cop drove past the filling station with the hammer down. Gas was only 26 cents and I never bought more then one dollar at a time — it would last one day.

The next day at the grocery store we were on a coffee break and a new member was there. After telling my story about how I got away from the cop, my boss walked over and said, do you no who that man is there? I said no! Well that's the cop. He started working part time. We became pretty good friends.

Paul had a gallon of ammonia and he said "here Mick, smell this." I took it out of his hands and smelled it. If you ever need your knees buckled and the feeling you lost the back of your head, you should try that sometime.

At 16 I started drinking like there was no tomorrow. No one could have told me that I would live past 21 years of age. Wayne, who worked at the grocery store and I would sometimes drink together. One night, after we drank too much, we decided to go visit his parents, who lived in Hot Springs. There was a blizzard in progress and driving down highway 79 about 10 p.m. there was several snow drifts across the road. When I saw one, I sped up and we slid through them and kept going. I saw one coming up that seemed higher then the rest, so I really pushed the gas down.

When the snow fell down and I could see out of the windshield, an 18 wheeler was in front of us. My buddy said, "I'll get out and push you backwards." So he got out with the wind blowing 40 to 50 miles an hour, put his back to the 18 wheeler, but the car never moved. He got back in the car and we went to sleep. The next morning the birds where out flying around in the sun shine. The temperature was 5 below 0 in the night. We caught a ride to Rapid City and had someone drive us back to get the car. It was one of two times that I was stranded in a car at -5 below. The next time was near Casper, Wyoming, when I went rabbit hunting.

Driving back from Hot Springs another time, Wayne and I went swimming. I was driving too fast and the car started sliding side ways around a curve.

The door came open and Wayne went out, the door. With his feet still in the car he was hanging on to the door handle and the post. The only thing that saved him was that I decided to turn the wheel and went straight out into the pasture. The momentum shifted and he was able to get back in the car. Without stopping I drove back onto the road.

I worked at the grocery store six years, part time, while I went to school. To give me more drinking money, I took industrial relations, starting in the 11th grade, where I had a class in the morning and worked all afternoon. That really left me a lot of time for real school.

In the 11th grade I discovered sex, with bar girls, and never went to the prom. Some days I would go from motel rooms to my class. Mom would lay awake all night waiting for me to come home. I personally put every gray hair in her head. After graduating from high school, "with college never mentioned," I came over to Casper to live with Dad. We made a good duet together.

Dad's girlfriend had a sister that took a week's vacation and the second week on a Saturday night we got into an argument. I left and went drinking. When I came back to the trailer no one was home, so I made out the bed in the couch. It was the first night that it looked like I was going to sleep by myself.
I heard the three come in about a half hour after I laid down, but I was too drunk to resist when I heard Dad say, "why don't you sleep with us." In about two hours, the sister's husband came storming through the front door with a 22 rifle and there I was sleeping like a baby, as I was told the next morning.

Dad had a heating stove that had too many BTUs for the trailer. Usually 10 minutes after he turned it up in the morning he would have to open the door. Dad had a special way he threw it open. This morning was different, the door only went about eight inches and came back and slammed shut. He looked out the side window and my Lincolns front bumper was only about eight inches from the door.

Mickey R. Mullen

Another time I was asleep on the hideaway bed that took up most of the front room and for some reason known only to Dad, he set on my feet with his full body weight. I guess it was time to get up. We worked for a while together on the same job. He was a carpenter and I started out as a laborer and managed to get a job in the office. When he was laid off Dad borrowed enough money from me to get to Idaho Falls. I had to rent an apartment.

When my job ended the company was going to transfer me to Missouri. My car had developed transmission trouble. With a knock on the door, my pathetic friend had found two girls with a car. I got in the back seat, and we went and got two six packs of Beer. The girls decided to go home and they let Mr. Pathetic borrow their dad's car. We went to a bar where I purchased another couple of six packs of beer. It wasn't long before Mr. Pathetic was driving on the wrong side of the road and he smashed head on into another car. When the ambulance came I was laying on the fender having gone through the windshield. The next morning I woke up and an insurance, "slick" had me sign some papers. I was in the hospital 21 days.

Paul came from Rapid City; after he saw me, he never drove stupid again. Mom came a couple days later and brought a pair of pants. I cried. Dad came just before I got out of the hospital and we walked out in the hall way to sit on a love seat, where he went to sleep. Paul took me back to Rapid City and the party never did end. He was stationed at the Rapid City Air Base and had married a Japanese girl during the Korean War. He eventually married a girl in Scotland and his last wife was from the Philippines. He had 13 children—most of them legal. He says today that he is "a veteran of foreign women."

One day I told Mom that I saw little specks when I looked at white paper, so she made me an appointment with a optometrists. He examined my eyes and gave me a prescription to get filled at the drug store. He made me another appointment. I told Paul that evening and he took me to another optometrists. He told me I had cut my eyes in the car wreck and I would always have the specks—they were scars on my eye balls.

Mom always had to get up early because she was the breakfast cook. One morning she looked out side and their was an Indian girl laying on the front lawn under a man's overcoat. She came in my bedroom and woke me up and asked, "did you bring your girl friend home with you? We have one out on the front lawn."

In Rapid City I ran around with a guy that came over from Germany. One night we were in one of our favorite bars and a couple was there. They was fascinated about Hank coming over from Germany. We told them that I had just got off the plane from there, it really fired them up and they started buying us drinks. Because I just arrived, I didn't know any English. It never occurred to them that I never knew German either. I grunted through the night and smiled a lot. When they left after they closed the bar, I couldn't stand up. Hank came over and took me out to my car and I drove him home. When I got to Mom's house I crawled to my bed.

Hank and I decided to go to Dead Wood, South Dakota. At that time you went because of the houses of prostitution. When we got there they threw us out because we were drunk. Today their draw card is gambling and they closed up the cubicles. Not too many can say they were thrown out of a bar, whore house, and a Chinese restaurant.

On the way back to Rapid City, coming around a curve in the Black Hills, the 1950 Lincoln that I was driving started to slide sideways. It went about a block on solid snow and ice and eventually drifted off the road breaking off a state sign. The rear end slammed into the side of the ditch and curled it up, then it flipped around and hit the same ditch curling the front end. The back window went about a quarter of a block and was leaning on a fence, unbroken. Hank had gravitated to the back seat. We got out of the car and could barely stand up on the road as we started walking to Sturgis. We hitchhiked to Rapid City.

Dad happened to be working at the base so I asked him if he would pull the car home. He said okay. Hank came along. When we got to the car, we saw it was a mess. Dad said it looked like we flipped the car end over end, so Hank said that was what happened. To this day Paul still believes that is what happened. For some time I have tried to set the record straight, but no one believes me that we didn't end over end the car, but it sure looked like it.

Dad got a 50-foot rope out of the truck and we were off to Rapid City. He pulled us, as if the car wasn't attached to the end of it. Hank couldn't believe what was happening, and I just barely did. At stop signs he didn't care if the rope was tight or not. When we got it home, Hank said it was the worst ride he had ever been on.

Paul took the motor out of the car and put it in another 1950 Cosmopolitan Lincoln, it was a bit longer. In the 1950s, the cars were often hard to start—we never had 10-30 motor oil. Paul's car wouldn't start, so he asked me to give him a jump start with jumper cables. I drove up beside his car and said, "I don't know what the problem is. I never have trouble with my cars." He said, "you never shut your car off."

Hank for one reason or other never had a car. Dad had bought a 1949 Ford in Casper, Wyoming, and then came over to Rapid City to work. Two couples had attended a dance in Hermosa, South Dakota, with Dad as the driver. At the dance, it was one of these family affairs with no alcohol inside, so you had to drink out in the car. Evidently Dad had made too many trips out to the car. On the way back to Rapid City he rolled over. This was his forth roll over, previously he had rolled two Model Ts, and one Model A.

The roof was flat, so we used a four by four and a jack and jacked the roof up. Dad had paid $600 for it. He said, "Mick, do you want to buy the car? I'll sell it to you for $150." I said okay. The hood was the only part of the car without a dent. I drove the car for about two years and it was the fastest car in a block, at the school. When I speed shifted to second gear it left more rubber on the road, then in first gear. There was something special about the motor and transmission.

Hank one day drove a '49 Ford over to the grocery store to let me try it out. He was thinking about buying it. We took off and I speed shifted the car like I did mine. We walked back to the store and Hank phoned the used car company and told them where their car was parked.

I had just arrived at one of my favorite bars to dance and it came over the loud speaker that a car was burning up outside. The second time they announced it they said a blue Lincoln. That got my attention, when I went outside the fire department had my back seat out of the car and was hosing it down. I never did replace it Whoever set in the back had to sit on bare medal.

One time I had a car full of guys and it was the third time that night a cop stopped me. One of them from the back asked, "Now what did you do?" Only one time did I get put in jail for drunken driving, and that was a bum steer. It was easily thrown out of court. Something that has always confounded me: in the drunk tank, as it was called, there was about six guys laying on the floor. One of the bunks was empty, it didn't take much persuasion for me to make a claim for it. The next morning before I bailed myself out, we had two hard boiled eggs. My neighbor said, "You better save one of them for later." I highly recommend that before high school graduation, every boy should be kept all night in a jail cell.

Three years later, one day, out of the blue, Mom said "why don't you go into the Air Force?" By this time I don't think she cared what color it was. I joined the Navy the same day; I got a penicillin shot for gonorrhea. When the Navy weighed me "with only the radio on" I weighed 125 pounds. I was 22 years old. The party had just gotten started.

It was not long before Mom wrote me that Murphy (her boyfriend) had been sober two years, so they got married. Murphy started drinking again, shot his little toe off with my shot gun, and they got a divorce. Then he had a stroke, and couldn't talk, for a while she tried to take care of him at her house but it turned out to be too much work. After she married him again she got him admitted at the military hospital in Hot Springs, South Dakota.

Mickey R. Mullen

It turned out to be the best thing she ever did, because they gave me $600 a month of a $3000 bill that Mom had when I eventually had to put her in a nursing home. Murphy was a veteran of World War II.

In Hawaii, my first duty station, my girlfriend and I couldn't find a motel room. I asked the taxi driver if he could use a cup of coffee. It was just what he needed. We got married after she told me she was pregnant. At the end of the first enlistment of four years we got a divorce. We probably lived together a total of six months, the rest of the time I was at sea or a port city.

Mickey home on leave, 1962.

Re-enlisting as a second class machinist mate, in Denver, where I received my physical. The person in charge told me to drop my pants, turn around, bend over, and spread my cheeks. I have often wondered about that "examination." After my physical examination I went down town and was walking in front of a bar, close to the gutter. A black man came out and went by me. Another one came out of the same bar. The first one turned around and said, "go ahead and shoot," so he shot him three times.

On the second ship we went to San Francisco to put the ship in dry dock for a major overhaul. The captain decided to do us a favor, and he put our personal cars on the ship to take with us. The only problem was that at the time I didn't have a car. One of the sailors talked me into going to town with him, he was younger than 21 years of age. We found ourselves in Oakland, California. When we were ready to go back to the ship, crossing the Bay Bridge, a Volks Wagon had ran out of gas. Of course he ran into the back end of it. I looked over at him and said, "I think I'll go back to the ship now." So I got out and started walking to the big city. Shortly a car stopped and this couple asked me if I saw the accident? I never could figure out where they thought I came from in the middle of the Bay Bridge, in a sailor suit.

The first time I met Ben was in National City, California, in a bar. I ask him if he wanted to play a game of pool, after I ran the table we became good friends. He was stationed on the same ship. Ben would smuggle whiskey aboard the ship; I never did have the nerve. I just helped him drink it. One time we went back to a gun mount, with our water, bidders, and whiskey. Ben passed out in the compartment, it must have been the rocking of the ship, I never saw him do that before. We were 2000 miles in the ocean.

Our chief was the officer of the day one time and he was making a round of the ship. Outside of the work place of Ben's, we each had a drink in our hand. The chief said he wanted to smell it. He calmly walked over and poured it over the side and left. One of the sailors in the Philippines came down with syphilis and was restricted to the ship six to nine months. When he was cured, we happened to be back in Subic Bay, in the Philippines. He went on liberty and came down with another dose. AIDS wasn't a concern during that era. At the end of the second enlistment, I was first class machinist mate. On the ship I was in charge of the main engine room. My major duty stations was Hawaii about seven months. The rest of the time — about three years — was spent on the USS Carter Hall LSD 3, and four years on the USS Comstock LSD 19.

With a total of eight years in the Navy, I received two honorable discharges, three Bronze Stars, Expeditionary Medal, Vietnam Service Medal - with Device, and two good Conduct medals. I was discharged December 1, 1967.

Walking out the front gate, I got on a city bus, with all that I owned in a sea bag. Moving into a sleeping room in Long Beach, California, I bought a corporation, 33,000 shares, with me as the president, secretary, janitor, vice president, maintenance man, controller, manager, and change person. It consisted of a restaurant, fish market, automobile repair garage all leased. A five-stall car wash, that I wish was leased. It really impressed Dad, he drove all the way from Casper, Wyoming, to check it out. He sat out in front of the car wash in his car and counted the cars that came in. That evening when we found each other, he came in the room and said he never saw any cars at the car wash. Earlier I had taken the quarters out of the boxes, and put them on the bed. Dad said "you're lying." He stayed one night and left the next morning.

To save the corporation, two months later I went to work assembling drill presses in Los Angeles. The only thing I got out of the corporation was a college education by hard knocks.

Mickey's car wash, next door to the filling station.

Mickey R. Mullen

THE WAY, THE TRUTH, AND THE LIFE,
ST JOHN 14 v 6

What is the reason for so many church denominations and religions?

Today, you are looked upon with scorn if you don't embrace most all religions. This reflection comes from a lack of understanding, that Jesus tried to portray. In a perfect world, at the time of Christ, all other religions and beliefs were to cease.

St Matthew 11 v 13 *For all the prophets and the law prophesied until John.*

St John 1 v 4 *In him was life; and the life was the light of men. v 5 And the light shineth in darkness; and the darkness comprehended (to grasp mentally; understand;) it not.*

St Matthew 7 v 21 *Not every one that saith unto me, Lord, Lord, shall enter into the kingdom of heaven; but he that doeth the will of my Father which is in heaven. v 22 Many will say to me in that day, Lord, Lord, have we not prophesied in thy name? and in thy name have cast out devils? and in thy name done many wonderful works? v 23 And then will I profess unto them, I never knew you: depart from me, ye that work iniquity.*

(Does this sound familiar?) " Salvation " as we are told, is as easy as falling off a log, Is it? You be the judge: The scriptures that I use, most of them you won't here in your church (or have the same meaning).

St Matthew 7 v 13 & 14 *Enter ye in at the strait gate: for wide is the* *gate, and broad is the way, that leadeth to destruction, and many there be which go in thereat: Because strait is the gate, and narrow is the way, which leadeth unto life, and few there be that find it.*

The reason the King James version of the Bible is in existence is the way it is written.

St Matthew 11 v 25 - 27 *At that time Jesus answered and said, I thank thee, O Father, Lord of heaven and earth, because thou hast hid these things from the wise and prudent, and hast reveled them unto babes. Even so, Father: for so it seemed good in thy sight. All things are delivered unto me of my Father: and no man knoweth the Son, but the Father; neither knoweth any man the Father, save (except) the Son, and he to whomsoever the Son will reveal him.*

St John 12 v 48 - 50 *He that rejecteth me, and receiveth not my words, hath one that judgeth him: the word that I have spoken, the same shall judge him in the last day. v 49 for I have not spoken of myself; but the Father which sent me, he gave me a commandment, what I should say, and what I should speak. And I know that his commandment is life everlasting: whatsoever I speak therefore, even as the Father said unto me, so I speak.*

One time a preacher was using four to six different Bibles in one sermon. It is fearful for me to not print the verses of the Old King James Bible, word for word, punctuation, capital letter's etc., as it is written. I use a "Cruden's Complete Concordance," based on the Old King James Bible. How can one use a Concordance, of all the Bibles in existence? Do you care?

Psalm 111 v 10 *The fear of the Lord is the beginning of wisdom: a good understanding have all they that do his commandments: his praise endureth forever.*

St John 5 v 43 *I am come in my Father's name, and ye receive me not: if another shall come in his own name, him ye will receive.*

Jesus came and was not excepted, neither was the word understood, which is the worst part, but if another shall come in his own name (Paul, of the Acts) him ye will receive and the word that he will write, is what you WANT TO UNDERSTAND even if it is faults doctrine. (You say, yes but he died for his belief's) Is this something new? If you wanted people to believe in what you are writing down wouldn't you write QUOTE All scripture is given by inspiration of God.

St John 10 v 1-5 *Verily, verily, I say unto you, He that entereth not by the door into the sheepfold, but climbeth up some other way, the same is a thief and a robber. But he that entereth in by the door is the shepherd of the sheep. To him the porter openeth; and the sheep hear his voice: and he calleth his own sheep by name, and leadeth them out. And when he putteth forth his own sheep, he goeth before them, and the sheep follow him: for they know his voice. And a stranger will they not follow, but will flee from him: for they know not the voice of strangers.* (Paul)

Thomas Jefferson (1743-1826), who drafted the Declaration of Independence. Quote taken from the *Casper Star Tribune* (7/21/01), "He repudiated the writings of the Apostle Paul, whom he considered the (first corrupter of the doctrines of Jesus)." He determined this with his intelligence.

Two divinity collage presidents was talking to one another recently on TV. One of them said the two greatest men that ever lived was Moses and Paul. (verse 5 above) what about Jesus or St John—or whoever wrote the Gospel of John, My Bible tells me that we are not sure who wrote it. Without Saint John, my experience with salvation would have been extremely difficult because it is so much different then the other three Gospels.

St John 5 v 33 - 34 *Ye sent unto John, and he bare witness unto the truth. But I receive not testimony from man: but these things I say, that ye MIGHT be saved.*

(Now lets go to Romans, as it is usually portrayed.)

St Mark 1 v 8 (John speaking) *I indeed have baptized you with water: but he (Jesus) shall*
baptize you with the Holy Ghost.

St Matthew 24 v 5 *For many shall come in my name, saying, I am Christ; and shall deceive many.*

St John 8 v 38 *I speak that which I have seen with my Father: and ye do that which ye have seen with your father.*

Isaiah 55 v 8 *For my thoughts are not your thoughts, neither are your ways my ways, saith the Lord.*

Deuteronomy 31 v 29 (Moses is speaking to Israel) *For I know that after my death ye will utterly corrupt yourselves, and turn aside from the way; which I have commanded you; and evil will befall you in the latter days; because ye will do evil in the sight of the Lord, to provoke him to anger through the work of your hands.*

St Matthew 3 v 7 *But when he saw many of the Pharisees and Sadducees come to his baptism, he said unto them, O generation of vipers, who hath warned you to flee from the wrath to come?*

St Matthew 13 v 10 - 13 *And the disciples came, and said unto him, Why speakest thou unto them in parables? He answered and said unto them, Because it is given unto you to know the mysteries of the kingdom of heaven, but to them it is not given. Therefore speak I to them in parables: because they seeing see not; and hearing they hear not, neither do they understand.*

Where does it say that you must go to a divinity college to understand the words of Matthew, Mark, Luke, and John of the King James version. St John 12 v 48 (above)?

St Matthew 6 v 33 *But seek ye first the kingdom of God, and his righteousness; and all these things shall be added unto you.*

Jesus had an advantage in the fact that he spoke in parables, where I have to write plainly.

St John 8 v 47 *He that is of God hearth God's words: ye therefore hear them not, because ye are not of God.*

After I received the Holy Ghost I started understanding the four Gospels and not one minute before then. According to the Bible, do we waste our time devoted to political achievements? No.

St Matthew 22 v 17 - 21 *Tell us therefore, What thinkest thou? Is it lawful to give tribute unto Caesar, or not? But Jesus perceived their wickedness, and said, Why tempt ye me, ye hypocrites? show me the tribute money. And they brought unto him a penny. And he saith unto them, Whose is this image and superscription? They say unto him, Caesar's. Then saith he unto them, Render therefore unto Caesar the things which are Caesar's; and unto God the things which are God's.*

This would include school prayer. It's not important and it probably does more harm then good. You as a parent want the school to do it all: raise, discipline, educate, pray, manners, dress, groom, etc.. In the meantime, let me sit back and drink my beer. There will be a judgment.

For some time I have thought about death and the common funeral. I found out a person that was making a prearranged funeral and paying for it up front told the sales lady that he wanted a Bible and a umbrella placed in the casket with him. Don't ask me what for—neither one is going to be any help. If you haven't came to know Jesus before death, there is no hope afterward. If you think I'm wrong about this, you're going to have to show me in the four Gospels.

At a common funeral, is there anything that a pastor or whomever can say to get you to heaven? I came to the conclusion that it is a waste of time and money. So at my prearranged funeral, I am to be taken to a funeral home and then placed directly in a coffin and buried in the Veterans Cemetery, if Jesus doesn't return first.

I feel cremation is not a good idea, but there might not be any harm done. God is a powerful God. It says the sea will give up its dead to stand in judgment.

Revelation 20 v 13 *And the sea gave up the dead which were in it; and death and hell delivered up the dead which were in them: and they were judged every man according to their works.*

The only work that one can claim credit for, hast to come from God. Jesus did a work.

Revelation 20 v 14 - 15 *And death and hell were cast into the lake of fire. This is the second death. And whosoever was not found written in the book of life was cast into the lake of fire.*

St Matthew 8 v 21 - 22 *And another of his disciples said unto him, Lord suffer me first to go and bury my father. But Jesus said unto him, Follow me; and let the dead (who are they) bury their dead.*

St Matthew 12 v 46 - 50 *While he yet talked to the people, behold, his mother and his brethren stood without, desiring to speak with him. Then one said unto him, Behold, thy mother and thy brethren stand without, desiring to speak with thee. But he answered and said unto him that told him, Who is my mother? and who are my breathren? And he stretched forth his hand toward his disciples, and said, Behold my mother and my brethren. For WHOSOEVER shall do the will of my Father which is in heaven, the same is my brother, and sister, and mother.*

St Matthew 6 v 9 - 13 *After this manner therefore pray ye:* (The Lord's Prayer) *Our Father which art in heaven, Hallowed be thy name. Thy* *kingdom come thy will be done in earth, as it is in heaven. Give us this day our daily bread. And forgive us our debts, as we forgive our debtors. And lead us not into temptation, but deliver us from evil: For thine is the kingdom, and the power, and the glory, for ever. Amen.*

Proverbs 14 v 12 *There is a way which seemeth right unto a man; but the end thereof are the ways of death.*

Psalm 58 v 3 *The wicked are estranged from the womb: they go astray as soon as they be born, speaking lies.*

St Luke 11 v 19 - 20 *And if I by Be-el'-ze-bub cast out devils, by whom do your sons cast them out? therefore shall they be your judges. But if I with the finger of God cast out devils, no doubt the Kingdom of God is come upon you.*

LOVE? Between God and Man!

St John 17 v 22 *And the Glory which thou gavest me I have given them; that they may be one, even as we are one.* (Written the same as when two people get married.)

St Matthew 19 v 5 *And said, For this cause shall a man leave father and mother, and shall cleave to his wife: and they twain,* (TWO) *shall be one flesh.*

St John 17 v 23 - 26 *I in them, and thou in me, that they may be made perfect in one; and that the world may know that thou hast sent me, and hast loved them, as thou hast loved me. Father, I will that they also, whom thou hast given me, be with me where I am; that they may behold my glory, which thou hast given me: for thou lovedst me before the foundation of the world.* (God knew the beginning as well as the ending and every thing in between, he new the day that his Son would be born.) *O righteous Father, the world hath not known thee: but I have known thee, and these have known that thou hast sent me. And I have declared unto them thy* *name, and will declare it:* (today and eternity) *that the love wherewith thou hast loved me may be in them, and I in them.*

Inveritably, God's love for mankind most always, is in association with his SON, in scripture for the new dispensation but the Israelite will always be God's chosen people. As a generality love mentioned in the old testament has to do with them. They are still not released from the obligations of the four Gospels.

Genesis 6 v 6 - 7 *And it repented the Lord that he had made man on the earth, and it grieved him at his heart. And the Lord said, I will destroy man whom I have created from the face of the earth; both man, and beast, and the creeping thing, and the fowls of the air; for it repenteth me that I have made them.*

Today I here "God is a good God" and "Love." It doesn't make any sense when you read Genesis 6 v 7. God is first and foremost a God of the Law, Judgment, righteousness, etc.. This code paraphrasing I have one word. SO?

Jeremiah 31 v 31 - 32 *Behold the days come, saith the Lord, that I will make a new covenant with the house of Israel, and with the house of Judah. Not according to the covenant that I made with their fathers in the day that I took them by the hand to bring them out of the land of Egypt; which my covenant they brake, although I was a husband unto them, saith the Lord.*

St John 10 v 16 *And other sheep I have, which are not of this fold, them also I must bring, and they shall hear my voice; and there shall be one fold, and one shepherd.*

Jeremiah 31 v 33 *But this shall be the covenant that I will make with the house of Israel; After those days, saith the Lord, I will put my law in their inward parts, and write it in their HEARTS; and will be their God, and they shall be my people.*

Jeremiah 31 v 34 *And they shall teach no more every man his neighbor, and every man his brother, saying, Know the Lord: for they shall all know me, from the least of them unto the greatest of them, saith the Lord: for I will forgive their iniquity, and I will remember their sin no more.*

Exodus 31 v 18 *And he gave unto Mosses, when he had made an end of communing with him upon mount Si'-nai, two tables of testimony, tables of stone, written with the finger of God.*

St Matthew 5 v 8 *Blessed are the pure in heart: for they shall see God.*

St Matthew 3 v 8 *Bring forth therefore fruits meet (suitable) for repentance.*

Jeremiah 15 v 6 *Thou hast forsaken me, saith the Lord, thou art gone backward: therefore will I stretch out my hand against thee, and destroy thee. I am weary with REPENTING.* (Repent and turn, not on your life.)

From the age of 10 to 30 was the time I had to (bring forth therefore fruits for repentance) As the old timers put it: "sowing wild oats." The average person would look upon my life as a hopeless case. God knows what I went through and the fact that I never took drugs and never really bothered anyone but myself. When I was drunk to the point that I couldn't walk, my mind would always be clear. In other words, I always tried to do the right thing in the things that mattered most in God's eyes. It says He knows your heart, and that is what matters to me. What you think doesn't matter.

Mickey R. Mullen

Mickey before salvation, 1963.

Would you believe in less then a minute my attitude changed, my ducks were placed in a row: I quit swearing, smoking, drinking, and then fasted for three days, and celibate for the next 15 years? That's what the New Covenant did for me.

When I got out of the Navy in Long Beach, California, in about a year, with a business failing, living in a sleeping room, and with a wreck of a car, I was in a real estate broker's office. The brokers secretary asked me, "has God has been good to you?" I told her that I went to church when I was a kid. She gave me her church's address.

Going to three different churches in two months, I was seeking the Holy Spirit that I had felt as a child. My Dad was a preacher for about four years.

St John 16 v 25 - 29 *These things have I spoken unto you in proverbs: but* *the time cometh, when I shall no more speak unto you in proverbs, but I shall show you plainly of the Father. At that day ye shall ask in my name: and I say not unto you, that I will pray the Father for you: For the Father himself loveth you, because ye have loved me, and have believed that I came out from God (in your heart). I came forth from the Father, and am come into the world: again, I leave the world, and go to the Father. His disciples said unto him, Lo, now speakest thou plainly, and speakest no proverb.*

St Matthew 7 v 7 - 8 *Ask, and it shall be given you; seek, and ye shall find; knock, and it shall be opened unto you: For every one that asketh receiveth; and he that seeketh findeth; and to him that knocketh it shall be opened.*

St Matthew 5 v 6 *Blessed are they which do hunger and thirst after righteousness: for they shall be filled.* (From above.)

Psalm 51 v 10 *Create in me a clean heart, O God, and renew a right spirit within me.*

St Luke 16 v 15 *And he said unto them, Ye are they which justify yourselves before men; but God knoweth your hearts for that which is highly esteemed among men is abomination in the sight of God.*

Conviction

St John 6 v 44 *No man can come to me, except the Father which hath sent me draw him: and I will raise him up at the last day.*

St John 6 v 37 *All that the Father giveth me shall come to me; and him that cometh to me I will in no wise cast out.*

St John 14 v 1 - 7 *Let not your heart be troubled: ye believe in God, believe also in me. In my Father's house are many mansions: if it were not so, I would have told you. I go to prepare a place for you. And if I go and* *prepare a place for you, I will come again, and receive you unto myself; that where I am, there ye may be also. And whither I go ye know, and the way ye know. Thomas saith unto him, Lord, we know not whither thou goest; and how can we know the way? Jesus saith unto him, I am the way, the truth, and the life: no man cometh unto the Father, but by me. If ye had known me, ye should have known my Father also: and from henceforth ye know him, and have seen him.*

St John 1 v 14 *And the Word was made flesh, and dwelt among us, (and we beheld his glory, the glory as of the only begotten of the Father,) full of grace and truth.*

St John 14 v 20 - 21 *At that day ye shall know that I am in my Father, and ye in me: and I in you. He that hath my commandments, and keepeth them, he it is that loveth me: and he that loveth me shall be loved of my Father, and I will love him, and will manifest myself to him.*

St John 10 v 37 - 38 *If I do not the works of my father, believe me not. But if I do, though ye believe not me, believe the works: THAT YE MAY KNOW, and believe, that the Father is in me, and I in him.* (The Fathers plan of Salvation)

Without conviction of sins, by the Holy Spirit, there can be no salvation. (Directed by the Father.)

In the third church that I went to, in two months, the congregation was singing; "smile a while, and give your face a rest, raise your hands to the one you love the best, turn around and shake a hand and smile, smile, smile." A lady came up to me and ask me if I loved Jesus? I said " NO." In most churches I would have been saved if I said "Yes." At the end of the service, the convictive Spirit that I had been looking for "was there," and I went down to the alter.

St Matthew 18 v 1 - 4 *At the same time came the disciples unto Jesus, saying, Who is the greatest in the kingdom of heaven? And Jesus called a* *little child unto him, and set him in the midst of them, And said, Verly I say unto you, Except ye be CONVERTED, and become as little children, ye shall not enter into the kingdom of Heaven. Whosoever therefore shall humble himself as this little child, the same is greatest in the kingdom of heaven. "*

At the alter I asked God to help me. When I got up, most of the congregation was shaking my hand and was calling me "BROTHER." After leaving the church, I went to a gas station with a pay phone on the outside wall to call my mother. When my mother answered I told her that "I went to the alter." She asked me to pray for "Dad and Me."

At that instant, I believed that I could pray and heal her: she had a crippled leg since childhood from polio and later on rheumatoid arthritis.

Standing there, something hit me in my back and knocked my heart out of me to the right. The suit coat went limp, with my body feeling sunken. At first, it had occurred to me, I was shot. The impact was so great my right foot went forward a half step. Finding out my neck was stiff, out of the corner of the left eye I saw and felt a long stream of white misty light entering my back and my body was filling up. According to scripture, "replacing my heart." It is my belief that Jesus is talking about the born again experience in the following:

St Matthew 9 v 16 -17 *No man putteth a piece of new cloth unto an old garment, for that which is put in to fill it up taketh from the garment, and the rent (tear) is made worse. Neither do men put new wine into old bottles: else the bottles break, and the wine runneth out, and the bottles perish: but they put new wine into new bottles, and both are preserved.*

St John 16 v 12 - 13 *I have yet many things to say unto you, but ye cannot bear them now; v 13 Howbeit when he, the Spirit of truth, is come, he will guide you into all truth: for he shall not speak of himself; but whatsoever he shall hear, that shall he speak: and he will show you things to come.*

St Matthew 12 v 34 *O generation of Vipers, how can ye being evil, speak good things? for out of the abundance of the heart the mouth speaketh.*

The next Wednesday night in the church service at the testimonial part, I stood up and said "I never got saved at the alter last Sunday night, but became SAVED at a service station." That went over like a lead balloon.

St John 5 v 44 *How can ye believe, which receive honor one of another, and seek not the honor that cometh from God only?*

Ezekiel 11 v 19 - 20 *And I will give them one heart, and I will put a new spirit within you; and I will take the stony heart out of their flesh, and will give them a heart of flesh: That they may walk in my statutes, and keep mine ordinances, and do them: and they shall be my people, and I will be their God.*

Predestination, chosen, or whosoever? **Isaiah 44 v 1** *Yet now hear, O Jacob my servant; and Israel, whom I have chosen:*

St Mark 13 v 20 *And except that the Lord had shortened those days, no flesh should be saved: but for the elect's sake, WHOM HE HATH CHOSEN, he hath shortened the days.*

St Matthew 20 v 16 *So the last shall be first, and the first last: for many be called, but few chosen.*

St Matthew 22 v 14 *For many are called, but few are chosen. St Luke 6 v 13 And when it was day, he called unto him his disciples: and of them he chose twelve, whom also he named apostles;*

St John 13 v 18, 20 *I speak not of you all: I know whom I have chosen: but that the scripture may be fulfilled, He that eateth bread with me hath lifted up his heel against me. Verily, verily, I say unto you, He that receiveth whomsoever I send receiveth me; and he that receiveth me* *receiveth him that sent me.*

St John 15 v 18 – 19 *If the world hate you, ye know that it hated me before it hated you. If ye were of the world, the world would love his own: but because ye are not of the world, but I have chosen you out of the world, therefore the world hateth you.*

If I was chosen as the most admired man in the United States, this verse would bother me. Amen; means you agree with what is said, it doesn't mean what is being said is the truth. Predestination and/or chosen. I was predestined before being born. This shouldn't be any surprise to anyone. Doesn't it say every hair on your head is numbered?

St Matthew 10 v 30 *But the very hairs of your head are all numbered.*

St John 2 v 19 - 21 *Jesus answered and said unto them, Destroy this temple, and in three days I will raise it up. Then said the Jews, Forty and six years was this temple in building, and wilt thou rear it up in three days?* (a Divinity college graduate) *But he spake of the temple of his body.* If Jesus chooses you out of this world, as the scripture suggest, then I can't think of any other way he dose it, " but the way you conduct your lives."

Proverbs 22 v 1 - 2 *A GOOD name is rather to be chosen than great riches, and loving favor rather than silver and gold. The rich and poor meet together: the Lord is the maker of them all.*

If Jesus' Body is a Temple, what about our bodies? It disgusts me for this reason when I see tattoo's and other paraphernalia. Let's hope that it only upsets me and not God. It could be "the rite of passage"—I believe that's the expression I have heard.

St Mark 13 v 20 *And except that the Lord had shortened those days, no flesh should be saved: but for the elect's sake, whom he hath chosen, he hath shortened the days.*

St John 3 v 16 This verse is not biblical, in relation to the rest of the four Gospels, and the way it is presented by the Preacher's. (How often, in the four Gospels, dose Jesus repeat himself, as in **St John 3 v 15 - 16**) *That whosoever believeth in him (in your heart) should not perish, but have eternal life.* (My Dad used to say he didn't chew his tobacco twice) *For God so loved the world, that he gave his only begotten Son, that whosoever believeth in him should not perish, but have everlasting life.*

Genesis 6 v 6 *And it repented the Lord that he had made man on the earth, and it grieved him at his heart.*

Can you comprehend the beauty of this world without man?

St Matthew 1 v 21 *And she shall bring forth a son, and thou shalt call his name Jesus: for he shall save his people from their sins.*

 St John 3 v 3 *Jesus answered and said unto him, Verily, verily, I say unto thee, Except a man be born again, he cannot see the kingdom of God.* (He cannot see the power of God.)

St Matthew 22 v 29 *Jesus answered and said unto them, Ye do err, not knowing the scriptures, nor the power of God.*

St Matthew 28 v 18 *And Jesus came and spake unto them, saying, All power is given unto me in heaven and in earth.*

St John 4 v 34 - 35 *Jesus saith unto them, My meat* (the reason that I'm here) *is to do the will of him that sent me, and to finish his work.* (Creation has never stopped.) If we want to consider the inventions and knowledge God has given to individuals. Evolution — — — — — — —NUTS— — — — — — —. *Say not ye, There are yet four months, and then cometh harvest? behold, I say unto you, Lift up your eyes, and look on the fields; for they are white already to harvest.*

St John 14 v 20 *at that day ye shall know that I am in my Father, and ye* *in me, and I in you. I believed the works that Jesus did. Their is some that may only have to (somehow) Believe me that I am in the Father, and the Father is in me or else believe me for the very works' sake*

St John 14 v 11. St Luke 11 v 20 *But if I with the finger of God cast out devils, (and or sin) no doubt the kingdom of God is come upon you.* It took 30 days for my body and mind to be cleaned up to receive the Holy Ghost. (I'm not talking about speaking in other tongues, that is of the Devil) voodoo worshipers has this same dialogue.

St Mark 16 v 17 *And these signs shall follow them that believe; In my name shall they cast out devils; they shall speak with new tongues*; The only time tongues (as a phenomenon) is recorded in the four Gospels. If it's suppose to be there, it could mean a new message, the good news or the word for the new testament age. (This dispensation.)

St Luke 4 v 1 *And Jesus being full of the Holy Ghost returned from Jordan, and was led by the Spirit into the wilderness,*

St Matthew 3 v 16 *And Jesus, when he was baptized, went up straightway out of the water: and, lo, the heavens were opened unto him, and he saw the Spirit of God descending like a dove, and lighting upon him*: (It went down his mouth and spread throughout his body.)

Exodus 16 v 14 *And when the dew that lay was gone up, BEHOLD, upon the face of the wilderness there lay a small round thing, as small as the hoar frost on the ground.*

One Sunday morning, 30 days after my born again experience, I went to a different church (this was the fourth church I'd been to, and it was a Protestant one.). The Pastor asked everyone to stand, and as we where singing a song, some force knocked the song book out of my hand to the floor. With no control of myself, I started walking down to the front of the church. The next sensation that I felt was the Pastor and another man's fingers digging in my sides, with me standing, and my arms out stretched.

Going back to my seat I felt under conviction (tearful) during the service and all the rest of that day, including the evening service.

The next morning I got up in my sleeping room and left, in my wreck of a car, to go to work. In a couple of miles I had a vision of a preacher on his knees that had left " one of the churches to evangelize."

Ezekiel 8 v 4; Daniel 8 v 1 & 2; Luke 1 v 22; I yelled out loud, " God help that Boy," when I got to BOY there was a white object, as a dove came through the windshield and went down my mouth and throat and spread throughout my body.

St John 1 v 32 - 33 *And John bare record, saying, I saw the Spirit descending from heaven like a dove, and it abode upon him. And I knew him not: but he that sent me to Baptize with water, the same said unto me, Upon whom thou shalt see the Spirit descending, AND REMAINING ON HIM, the same is he which baptizeth with the Holy Ghost.*

St Luke 12 v 50 *But I have a baptism to be baptized with; and how am I straitened* (burdened or to finish) *till it be accomplished !*

St John 14 v 26 *But the Comforter, which is the Holy Ghost, whom the Father will send in my name, he shall teach you all things, and bring all things to your remembrance, whatsoever I have said unto you.*

St John 15 v 26 *But when the Comforter is come, whom I will send unto you from the Father, even the Spirit of truth, which proceedeth from the Father, he shall testify of me:*

St John 3 v 27 *John answered and said, A man can receive nothing, except it be given him from heaven.*

St John 3 v 30 *He must increase, but I must decrease.*

St John 17 v 8, 25 *For I have given unto them the words which thou gavest me; and they have received them, and have known surely that I came out from thee, and they have believed that thou didst send me. O righteous Father, the world hath not known thee: but I have known thee, and these have known that thou hast sent me.*

After receiving the Holy Ghost, it was the second time that I was forced to fast for three days. Listening to as much church programming on TV, radio, and going to church, I noticed that the preachers was staying away from the four Gospels as much as they could, and nothing was making any sense to me. It didn't take me long to decide to listen, and compare not only what occurred to me but what the four Gospels was all about. At first also the Holy Ghost made me feel nauseated every time I started reading the Book of Acts. Since then, I have only read the Old Testament, Four Gospels, and Revelation of the King James Version of the Bible, but have a working knowledge (the Preachers) of the rest of the New Testament.

St Matthew 20 v 20 -23 *Then came to him the mother of Zeb'-e-dee's children with her sons, worshiping him, and desiring a certain thing of him. And he said unto her, What wilt thou? She saith unto him, Grant that these my two sons may sit, the one on thy right hand, and the other on the left, in thy kingdom. But Jesus answered and said, Ye know not what ye ask, are ye able to drink of the cup that I shall drink of, and to be baptized with the baptism that I am baptized with? They say unto him, We are able. And he said unto them, Ye shall drink indeed of my cup, and be baptized with the baptism that I am baptized with: but to set on my right hand, and on my left, is not mine to give, but it shall be given to them for whom it is prepared of my Father.* BAPTISM OR BAPTIZED, BAPTIZETH: Doesn't always mean sprinkling or full body, emerging in water.

St John 3 v 5 *Jesus answered, Verily, verily,* (Its time to pay attention) *I say unto thee, Except a man be born of water* (not H_2O) *and of the Spirit,* (not Wine but the Holy Ghost) *he cannot ENTER into the kingdom of God. Remember v 3 was see and here it is enter. I saw and felt,* (the power) *of* *the Lord and when receiving the Holy Ghost Entered into the Kingdom of God.*

St Matthew 4 v 4 *Man shall not live by bread alone, but by every word that proceedeth out of the mouth of God.* (Jesus)

St John 8 v 28 *Then said Jesus unto them, When ye have lifted up the Son of man, then shall ye know that I am he, and that I do nothing of myself; but as my Father hath taught me, I SPEAK THESE THINGS.*

St Mark 13 v 22 *For false Christs and false prophets shall rise, and shall show signs and wonders, to seduce, if it were possible, even the elect.* (It is not possible to fool the Elect).

St John 10 v 5 *And a stranger will they not follow, but will flee from him: for they know not the voice of strangers. v 4 And when he putteth forth his own sheep, he goeth before them, and the sheep follow him: for they know his voice.* Father never means "Pope."

St Matthew 23 v 9 *And call no man your father upon the earth: for one is your Father, which is in heaven.* Did St Matthew, an Apostle, and the other three writers of the four Gospels ever really understand what they were writing down? { the Apostles thought He was coming back in their life-time, but they did understand that He was, "the Christ."

St Matthew 16 v 16 *And Simon Peter answered and said, Thou art the Christ, the Son of the living God.* Did Peter ever show a real understanding of what Jesus was all about?

St Luke 24 v 45 *Then opened he their understanding that they might understand the scriptures.* Why do I question this verse?

St John 14 v 26 *But the Comforter, which is the Holy Ghost, whom the Father will send in my name, he shall teach you all things, and bring all* *things to your remembrance, whatsoever I have said unto you.*

St John 16 v 7 *Nevertheless I tell you the truth; It is expedient for you that I go away: for if I go not away, the Comforter will not come unto you; but if I depart, I will send him unto you. (above) The Born again experience and receiving the Comforter made it possible for my body to bear the truth.*

St Luke 24 v 45 *Then opened he their understanding, that they might understand the scriptures,* It is my opinion that St John 16 v 7 (above) and St Luke 24 v 45 contradict each other.

St John 4 v 31- 32 *In the meanwhile his disciples prayed (urged) him saying, Master eat. But he said unto them, I have meat to eat that ye know not of.* A Man on T V was explaining how God is all three in one, God, Jesus, and the Holy Ghost, all of the scripture's, was in Genesis, with one exception, he used one verse in St John. (another hour wasted) (another book to be ordered) (another bid for MOO LAW). God said, the only way to salvation is to believe on or in his Son whom he truly loves. In the old testament Jesus was only a figment of imagination that was to come to pass. If these next verses don't convenience you, that the three are separate, then I would say there is no hope for you.

St John 8 v 29 *And he that sent me is with me: the Father hath not left me alone; for; I do always those things that please him.*

Revelation 5 v 1 - 5 *And I saw in the right hand of him (God) that sat on the throne a book written within and on the backside, sealed with seven seals. And I saw a strong angel proclaiming with a loud voice, Who is worthy to open the book, and to loose the seals thereof? And no man in heaven, nor in earth, neither under the earth, was able to open the book, neither to look thereon. And one of the elders saith unto me, Weep not: behold, the Lion of the tribe of Judah, the Root of David, hath prevailed to open the book, and to loose the seven seals thereof. (Jesus Christ.)*

St Mark 12 v 32 -34 *And the scribe said unto him, Well, Master, thou hast said the truth: for there is one God;* (yes) *also Jesus the Son and the Holy Ghost. and there is none other but he: And to love him with all the heart, and with all the understanding, and with all the soul, and with all the strength, and to love his neighbor as himself, is more than all whole burnt offerings and sacrifices. And when Jesus saw that he answered discreetly, he said unto him, THOU ART NOT FAR FROM THE KINGDOM OF GOD. And no man after that durst* (dared) ask him any question. (It's my belief that the scribe was being scornful.)

Bringing you up to the present, what has taken place? I came under the Conviction, was Saved (converted) at a gas station, and 30 days later received the Holy Ghost in my moving car. What next? What happened to Jesus? Didn't he say that "Ye shall drink indeed of my cup." Satan rebelled against God.

Isaiah 14 v 12 - 14. *How art thou fallen from heaven, O Lucifer, son of the morning ! how art thou cut down to the ground, which didst weaken the nations ! For thou hast said in thine heart, I will ascend into heaven, I will exalt my throne above the stars of God: I will sit also upon the mount* (all) *of the congregation,* (churches and Religions) *in the sides of the north:* If you think Satan is down at the bar, you're sadly mistaken. *I will ascend above the heights of the clouds; I will be like the most High.*

St Matthew 4 v 1 - 11 T*hen was Jesus led up of the Spirit (Holy Ghost) into the wilderness to be tempted of the devil.* This was the time that God would know if Jesus would be loyal, to him, or to Satan, as Satan had rebelled against him. After receiving the Holy Ghost my life became a night mare (boot camp) if it was the same, with Jesus, then not only was Jesus tempted of the Devil but it was a time of learning, (Holy Ghost) with me it lasted two years.

St Matthew 4 v 2 - 7 *And when he had fasted forty days and forty nights, he was afterward ahungered.* My Fast, lasted only three days. Jesus fasted

40 days, and it doesn't say how long he was in the wilderness. *And when the tempter came to him,* (How does this occur? When you can answer this question no doubt the Kingdom of Heaven has come upon you.) (You must plead, Jesus name) he said, *If thou be the Son of God, command that these stones be made bread. (above) Then the devil taketh him up into the holy city,* (Devils domain) *and setteth him on a pinnacle of the temple, And saith unto him, If thou be the Son of God, cast thyself down: for it is written, He shall give his angels charge concerning thee: and in their hands they shall bear thee up, lest at any time thou dash thy foot against a stone. Jesus said unto him, It is written again, Thou shalt not tempt the Lord thy God.*

St Mark 16 v 18 Should not be in the Bible as it is written. *They shall take up serpents; and if they drink any deadly thing, it shall not hurt them; they shall lay hands on the sick, and they shall recover.* (Would Jesus harass one of Gods creations?)

St Matthew 4 v 8 - 11 *Again, the Devil taketh him up into an exceeding high mountain, and showeth him all the kingdoms of the world,* (inventions) *and the glory of them; And saith unto him, All these things will I give thee, if thou will fall down and worship me. Then saith Jesus unto him, Get thee hence, Satan: for it is written, Thou shalt worship the Lord thy God, and him only shalt thou serve. Then the Devil leaveth him, and, behold, angels came and ministered unto him.*

Graduation. (Jesus begins his ministry according to the book of Matthew) It doesn't matter to me what you do in the life you are living, but you will answer to Jesus on the Day of Judgment.

St John 5 v 22 *For the Father judgeth no man, but hath committed all judgment unto the Son:* The important thing is, " however you are conducting your life; will he find you acceptable, in this dispensation, for his salvation." (If you are so righteous that you feel that you don't need to be converted, you are in the most dangerous situation of all, next to those that have there own brand of religion.)

St Mark 8 v 36 - 37 *for what shall it profit a man, if he shall gain the whole world, and lose his own soul? Or what shall a man give in exchange for his soul?* One Sunday in Sunday school, (fifth church) the teacher had the task of teaching the lesson in St John 2 v 1-12. Toward the end, after another wasteful session and two years after being saved, I looked up and saw an Angel (pure white) sort of like a female graduation uniform and I couldn't recall any hands, feet or head. I said the Day of Judgment was Coming, as it disappeared.

St Matthew 4 v 11 (above) I didn't know it at the time but my two-year ordeal was over, "it was my graduation." 11 January 1970. That evening, not going to the service, I was reading in my Bible at midnight, it was about time to go to bed because of my job in the morning. Going to the kitchen for a glass of water in a audible voice, it said "change the water into wine." At first, it was hard for me to believe what I just heard. Not costing me anything, I filled up the glass with water and took it in the living room, setting it on the coffee table.

Raising both arms toward heaven I said, "My Father, which art in heaven, change the water into wine in Jesus name." Nothing happened in the glass, it occurred in my body, there was a sensation from my fingers to my toes. Afterward it felt like my height had been reduced. Where would you go if you thought that occurred to you? I went to the bath room and looked in the mirror.

St John 2 v 1 - 12 (abbreviated) v 1 —a marriage v 2 —both Jesus and his disciples were called v 3 — Mother said they have no wine (notice it is a small letter) v 4 — *mine hour is not yet come* v 5 — *whatsoever he saith unto you do it.* v 6 —-*six water pots of stone,(containing two or three firkins apiece)* (perhaps the weight of water in the average Body of a Male or Female) v 7 —-*Fill the water pots with water* v 8 —-*Draw out now,* v 9 *When the ruler of the feast had tasted the water that was made wine, and knew not whence it was: But the Servants which drew the water knew;* (it is my belief that the water [wine] came from the Body of Jesus or from above) *the governor of the feast called the bridegroom,* v 10 *And saith unto him, Every man at the beginning doth set forth good wine; and when men have well drunk, then that which is worse*: (here is he talking about Sin and the products of it) *but thou hast kept the good Wine until now.* (Salvation) v11 *This beginning of miracles did Jesus in Cana of Galilee, and manifested forth his glory; and his disciples believed on him* v 12 — Went to Caper'-na-um. In chapter 6 of St John It is written in an allegory manner and yet some of it actually happened. (A story in which things, have another meaning) (part of Jesus speaking in parables)

St John 6 v 31 - 41 *Our Fathers did eat man'-na in the desert; as it is written, He gave them bread from heaven to eat. Then Jesus said unto them, Verily, verily, I say unto you, Moses gave you not that bread from heaven; but my Father giveth you the true bread from heaven. For the bread of God is he which cometh down from heaven, and giveth life unto the World. Then said they unto him, Lord, evermore give us this bread. And Jesus said unto them, I am the bread of life: he that cometh to me shall never hunger; and he that believeth on me shall never thirst. But I said unto you, That ye also have seen me, and believe not. All that the Father giveth me shall come to me; and him that cometh to me I will no wise cast out. For I came down from heaven, not to do mine own will, but the will of him that sent me. And this is the Father's will which hath sent me, That of all which he hath given me I should lose nothing, but should raise it up again at the last day. And this is the will of him that sent me, that every one which seeth the Son,* (St John 3 v 3 above) *and believeth on him,* (Land Mine) *may have everlasting life: and I will raise him up at the last day. The Jews then murmured at him, because he said, I am the bread which came down from heaven.*

St Luke 16 v 31 *And he said unto him, If they hear not Moses and the prophets, neither will they be persuaded, though one rose from the dead.*

St John 5 v 46 - 47 *For had ye believed Moses, ye would have believed me: for he wrote of me. But if ye believe not his writings, how shall ye believe my words?*

St John 6 v 42 - 49 *And they said, Is not this Jesus, the Son of Joseph, whose father and mother we know? how is it then that he saith, I came down from heaven? Jesus therefore answered and said unto them, Murmur not among yourselves. No man can come to me, except the Father which hath sent me draw him: and I will raise him up the last day It is written in the prophets, And they shall be all taught of God, Every man therefore that hath heard, and hath learned of the Father, cometh unto me. v 46 Not that any man hath seen the Father, SAVE HE WHICH IS OF GOD, HE HATH SEEN THE FATHER. Verily, verily, I say unto you, He that believeth on me hath everlasting life,* (Land Mine) *I am that bread of life. Your fathers did eat man'-na in the wilderness, and are dead.*

Exodus 16 v 12 - 15 *I have heard the murmurings of the children of Israel: speak unto them, saying, At even ye shall eat flesh, and in the morning ye shall be filled with bread; and ye shall know that I am the Lord your God. And it came to pass, that at even the quails came up, and covered the camp: and in the morning the dew lay round about the host. And when the dew that lay was gone up, behold, upon the face of the wilderness there lay a small round thing, as small as the hoar frost on the ground. And when the children of Israel saw it, they said one to another, It is man'-na: for they wist not what it was And Mosses said unto them, This is the bread which the Lord hath given you to eat.* (I have no trouble, believing that this took place) bread, flesh or meat born again, quail (blood) drink indeed, Holy Ghost.

St John 6 v 50 - 58 *This is the bread which cometh down from heaven, that a man may eat thereof, and not die. I am the living bread which came down from heaven: if any man eat of this bread, he shall live forever: and the bread that I will give is my flesh, which I will give for the life of the world. The Jews therefore strove(argued) among themselves, saying, How can this man give us his flesh to eat? Then Jesus said unto them, Verily, verily, I say unto you, Except ye eat the flesh of the Son of man, and drink his blood, ye have no life in you. Whoso eateth my flesh, and drinketh my blood, hath eternal life; and I will raise him up at the last day. For my* *flesh is meat indeed, and my blood is drink indeed. He that eateth my flesh, and drinketh my blood, dwelleth in me, and I in him. As the living Father hath sent me, and I live by the Father: so he that eateth me, even he shall live by me. This is that bread which came down from heaven: NOT AS YOUR FATHERS DID EAT MAN'NA AND ARE DEAD: HE THAT EATETH OF THIS BREAD SHALL LIVE FOREVER.*

St John 3 v 5 (above) **St John 6 v 59** *These things said he in the syna-gogue, as he taught in Ca-per'-na-um.*

Revelation 2 v 17 *He that hath an ear, let him hear what the Spirit saith unto the churches; To him that overcometh will I give to eat of the hidden man'na, and will give him a white stone, (those who were acquitted in Judgment) and in the stone a new name written, which no man knoweth saving he that receiveth it.*

With out God's intervention, there is no hope that I can see at this time. False doctrine is running rampant and THEY have made it EASY in their salvation. When it is easy, "a line will form," but salvation was the most difficult thing that I have ever accomplished in my lifetime. The simple reason, one is dealing with the unseen, and the faults doctrine of the leaders. Most all the churches, if you care to ask, will tell you we have one thing that man hasn't distorted, over populated, polluted, damaged, stolen, disrupted, neglected, defaced, self-seeker, lied, corrupted, backbiter, wasteful, greed, but the Bible is true, cover to cover. In the book of Joel we find the only hope to turn this dispensation around.

Joel 2 v 28 - 32 *And it shall come to pass afterward, that I will pour out my spirit upon all flesh; and your sons and your daughters shall prophesy, your old men shall dream dreams, your young men shall see visions: And also upon the servants and upon the handmaids in those days will I pour out my spirit. And I will show wonders in the heavens and in the earth, blood, and fire, and pillars of smoke. The sun shall be turned into dark-ness, and the moon into blood, before the great and the terrible day of the Lord come. And it shall come to pass, that whosoever shall call on the name of the lord shall be delivered: for in mount Zion and in Jerusalem* *shall be deliverance, as the lord hath said, and in the remnant whom the Lord shall call.*

You are the only one who can answer the question. "Is my religion founded on sound doctrine?" What took place 2000 years ago. Jesus was born, (who was the Son of God). He did miracles that convinced everyone around him that he was the Son of God, gave us the word, and died on the cross for our sins (because of the purity of God) and rose again.

St Matthew 18 v 11 *For the Son of man is come to save that which was lost.*

St Mark 7 v 9 *And he said unto them, Full well ye reject the commandment of God, that ye may keep your own tradition.*

St Matthew 12 v 37 *For by thy words* (your words) *thou shalt be justified, and by thy words* (your words) thou shalt be condemned.

St Matthew 15 v 18 *But those things which proceed out of the mouth come forth from the heart; and they defile the man.*

St Matthew 13 v 35 *That it might be fulfilled which was spoken by the prophet, saying, I will open my mouth in parables; I will utter things which have been kept secret from the foundation of the world.*

St Matthew 23 v 28 *Even so ye also outwardly appear righteous unto men, but within ye are full of hypocrisy and iniquity.*

St John 7 v 24 *Judge not according to the appearance, but judge righteous judgment.*

St Luke 6 v 40 *The disciple is not above his master: but everyone that is perfect shall be as his master.*

St Matthew 20 v 23 (above) *Ye shall drink indeed of my cup, and be baptized with the baptism that I am baptized with.*

St John 20 v 17 *Jesus saith unto her, Touch me not; for I am not yet ascended to my Father: but go to my brethren, and say unto them, I ascend unto my Father, and your Father; and to my God, and your God.*

Does it make any common sense, to you, that men preach from the Old Testament and the books of the New Testament (excluding) Revelation, and the four Gospels, 98 percent of the time?

Jesus gave us the Word, so I have only used the four Gospels 98 percent of the time, which makes more common sense to you. It is unbelievable what men have concocted and gullible people have believed.

St John 16 v 20 *Verily, verily, I say unto you, that Ye shall weep and lament,* (that's me) *but the world shall rejoice*: (Isn't that the truth) *and ye shall be sorrowful, but your sorrow shall be turned into joy. (yet we sing of Joy, unspeakable,) I am sorrowful but not for myself.*

St John 11 v 35 *Jesus wept.* (Most of the time we don't weep because of the here and now, but either what happened in the past, or something that will happen in the future.) (With the love of God in you, you will weep.) When Jesus prayed in secret, you can bet at each place he left tears on the ground.

St John 6 v 26 *Jesus answered them and said, Verily, verily I say unto you, Ye seek me, not because ye saw the miracles, but because ye did eat of the loves, and were filled.* (How can one change his Doctrine, with hundreds, thousands, and millions believing in you, and the commitment's that one has made?)

St Matthew 23 v 23 *Woe unto you, scribes and Pharisees, hypocrites! for ye pay tithe of mint and anise and cumin, and have omitted the weightier* *matters of the law, judgment, mercy, and faith: these ought ye to have done, and not leave the other undone.*

St Matthew 23 v 14 *Woe unto you, scribes and Pharisees, hypocrites! for ye devour widows' houses, and for a pretense make long prayer: therefore ye shall receive the greater damnation.* All of St Matthew chapter 23 is interesting. I guess it's which side of the fence you're on.

One would rather be lost than admit there is something wrong, "your common sense should reveal it to you." Was Jesus Christ lying when He said that He was the Son of God and we would be judged by the word that the Father gave Him, to reveal to us?

What about **St John 3 v 27**? John answered and said, *A man can receive nothing, except it be given him from heaven.* This was John the Baptist speaking, the one that was baptizing in water and there is other similar verses.

St Luke 20 v 34 *And Jesus answering said unto them, The children of this world marry, and are given in marriage: v 35 But they which shall be accounted worthy to obtain that world, and the resurrection from the dead, neither marry, nor are given in marriage: v 36 Neither can they die any more: for they are equal unto the angels; and are the children of God, being the children of the resurrection.*

Celebration of the New Dispensation

St Matthew 26 v 26 - 29 *And as they were eating, Jesus took bread, and blessed it, and brake it, and gave it to the disciples, and said Take, eat; this is my body. And he took the cup, and gave thanks, and gave it to them, saying, Drink ye all of it; For this is my blood of the new testament, which is shed for many for the remission of sins. But I say unto you, I will not drink henceforth of this fruit of the vine, until that day when I drink it new with you in my Father's kingdom.* (this was the end of it) (above) **St John**

6 v 31 - 58 (NOTHING HAS GOD REVEALED TO ME, AS BEING NECESSARY THAT MAN HAS TO DO IN THIS DISPENSATION AS A RITUAL, OR FOR SALVATION)

St Luke 18 V 26 - 27 *And they that heard it said, Who then can be saved? And he said, The things which are impossible with men are possible with God.*

St John 14 v 1 *Let not your heart be troubled: ye believe in God, believe also in me.*

St John 14 v 2 - 3 *In my Father's house are many mansions: if it were not so, I would have told you. I go to prepare a place for you. And if I go and prepare a place for you, I will come again, and receive you unto myself; that where I am, there ye may be also.* (First the elect will go up, then we will come back with Jesus and his Angels to rule 1000 years.)

Revelation 21 v 2 *And I John saw the holy city, new Jerusalem, coming down from God out of heaven, prepared as a bride adorned for her husband.* Some believe Jesus is going to put up a shack on this Earth.

St Luke 14 v 13 - 15 *But when thou makest a feast, call the poor, the maimed, the lame, the blind: And thou shalt be blessed; for they cannot recompense thee: for thou shalt be recompensed at the resurrection of the just. And when one of them that sat at meat with him heard these things, he said unto him, Blessed is he that shall eat bread in the kingdom of God.*

(St John 6 v 48- 51 & 3 v 3) **St Luke 14 v 16 - 21** *Then said he unto him, A certain man made a great supper, and bade many: v 17 And sent his servant at suppertime to say to them that were bidden, Come; for all things are now ready. And they all with one consent began to make excuse. The first said unto him, I have bought a piece of ground,* (Mortgaged to my eye balls) *and I must needs go and see it: I pray thee have me excused. v 19 And another said, I have bought five yoke of oxen, and I go to prove them: I pray thee have me excused. v 20 And another said, I have married* *a wife, and therefore I cannot come. v 21 So that servant came, and showed his lord these things. Then the master of the house being* angry (Genesis 6 v 7) *said to his servant, Go out quickly into the streets and lanes of the city,* (until about 1900 most people lived on a Farm) *and bring in hither the poor, and the maimed, and the halt, and the blind. v 22 And the servant said, Lord, it is done as thou hast commanded, and yet there is room.*

Malachi 4 v 5 *Behold, I will send you E-li'-jah the prophet before the coming of the great and dreadful day of the Lord.*

St Luke 14 v 23 – 24 *And the lord said unto the servant, Go out into the highways* (expression used since 1900) *and hedges, and compel them to come in, that my house may be filled. For I say unto you, That none of those men which were bidden shall taste of my supper.*

St Matthew 24 v 30 - 31 *And then shall appear the sign of the Son of man in heaven: and then shall all the tribes of the earth mourn, and they shall see the Son of man coming in the clouds of heaven with power and great glory. And he shall send his angels with a great sound of a trumpet, and they shall gather together his elect from the four winds, from one end of heaven to the other.*

Revelation 20 v 6 *Blessed and holy is he that hath part in the first resurrection: on such the second death hath no power, but they shall be priests of God and of Christ, and shall reign with him a thousand years.*

Because Jesus was who He was, couldn't say precisely what was on His mind, I'm sure He was extremely agitated in the unbelief, and misunderstanding of those around Him.

St John 12 v 14 - 15 *And Jesus, when he had found a young ASS, sat thereon; as it is written, Fear not, daughter of Zion: behold, thy King cometh, sitting on an ass's colt.*

St Matthew 23 v 15 *Woe unto you scribes and Pharisees, hypocrites! for ye compass (go over) sea and land to make one proselyte,* (a person who has been converted from one religion, or opinion to another) *Proselytize* (convert) *and when he is made, ye make him twofold more the child of hell than yourselves.*

Why did God save me outside the church buildings?

Joel 1 v 13 – 15 *Gird yourselves, and lament, ye priests: howl ye ministers of the alter: come, lie all night in sackcloth, ye ministers of my God: for the meat offering and the drink offering is withholden from the house of your God. Sanctify ye a fast, call a solemn assembly, gather the elders and all the inhabitants of the land into the house of the Lord your God, and cry unto the lord, Alas for the day! for the day of the Lord is at hand, and as a destruction from the almighty shall it come.*

Joel 2 v 1 *Blow ye the trumpet in Zion, and sound an alarm in my holy mountain: let all the inhabitants of the land tremble: for the day of the Lord cometh, for it is nigh at hand;*

Revelation 7 v 13 - 14 *And one of the elders answered, saying unto me, What are these which are arrayed in white robes? and whence came they? And I said unto him, Sir, thou knowest. And he said to me, These are they which came out of great tribulation, and have washed their robes, and made them white in the blood of the Lamb.*

What about the seven churches?

Revelation 2 v 7 EPHESUS (abbreviated) *—to him* (singular) *that overcometh will I give to eat of the tree of life, which is in the midst of the paradise of God* (Kingdom of God).

St John 3 v 3 SMYRNA v 9 - 10 *—and I know the blasphemy of them which say they are Jews, and are not, but are the synagogue of Satan. Fear none of those things which thou shalt suffer: behold, the devil shall* *cast some of you into prison, that ye may be tried; and ye shall have tribulation ten days: be thou faithful unto death, and I will give the a crown of life. —He that overcometh shall not be hurt of the second death.*

PERGAMOS v 14 *—them that hold the doctrine of Ba'-laam, —v 17 To him that overcometh will I give to eat of the hidden man'-na,*

THYATIRA v 20 *Notwithstanding I have a few things against thee.*

SARDIS 3 v 5 *He that overcometh, the same shall be clothed in white raiment; and I will not blot out his name out of the book of life, —.*

PHILADELPHIA v 12 *Him that overcometh —, and I will write upon him the name of my God, —.*

LAODICEA v 17, 20 - 21 *Because thou sayest, I am rich, and increased with goods, and have need of nothing; and knowest not that thou art wretched, and miserable, and poor, and blind, and naked: Behold, I stand at the door, and knock: if any man hear my voice, and open the door, I will* *come in to him, and will sup with him, and he with me. To him that overcometh —.*

Was God happy with any of them? NO. "You say, "He is talking about the church down the street! Waco, Heavens Gate, Guiana, New Age, snake handlers, bigamist, Falun Gong. God is not talking about Protestant, Morman, Catholic, Jewish, Baptist, Pentecostal, Uniterian, or Scientology?

My Bible tells me that Satan deceived the nations.

Revelation 20 v 1 - 3 *And I saw an angel come down from heaven, having the key of the bottomless pit and a great chain in his hand. And he laid hold on the dragon, that old serpent, which is the Devil, and Satan, and bound him a thousand years, And cast him into the bottomless pit, and shut him up, and set a seal upon him, that he should deceive the nations no more, till the thousand years should be fulfilled: and after that he must be loosed a little season.*

Please write to me:
Mickey Mullen
P.O. Box 1344
Casper, WY 82601

Mickey R. Mullen

My Life
Part 2

Dad used to ask, "Mick, are you ever going to amount to anything?" When I became successful, his hateful ways persisted. I always felt it was because of my association with Mom and their divorce. Perhaps she could have pulled it off by herself, I don't know. Remember she only had one good leg and never drove a car. All those years she could have driven an automatic shift.

After my conversion, I continued working at assembling drill presses, sold the corporation, and bought my first new car: a Volks Wagon.

My ex-wife had married another sailor and he was going to be transferred to Japan. I asked her for custody of our child, Mickey Mike, and she agreed.

He was half way thrrough the second grade; I moved from Long Beach to San Padro, California. After my spiritual graduation, the dog, child, clothes, and $1000 cash was put in the VW and we headed East.

I was parked in the drive way of Mom's house in Rapid City, South Dakota, when a taxi drove up and Mom got out. There was as much hate on her face as I had ever saw on a human being.

She asked us in, which for awhile I was not sure of. Her house needed painting and I started doing that. Slowly the ice started melting, and the child and I started going to church. He was the only reason that I went.

Mickey with son, Mickey Mike.

Since I'd done a lot of painting in the Navy, I was directed to the owner of a painting contractor. He asked me, "if I drank?" I said no and neither did I smoke or curse, either. The boss of the outfit the next morning was "cursing up a storm." I knew I was in trouble, but worked about two months.

One day Mom noticed an ad in a news paper for a carpentry class at Stevens Vocational School that would begin in the fall. Through the GI Bill, I got a few dollars for the school. I had to live with Mom at the age of 32! When the school got started, I worked part time at a gas station. A spiritual goal was always in the background, but never materialized until now. God has His own time schedule.

At graduation, I was the number one student of the class. Dad talked me into coming over to Casper, Wyoming, to take the exam for journeyman carpenter, which I passed easily.

Not too steady on my feet yet—it was only a year earlier that I drove my first nail, so I moved into Dad's trailer that we bought so long ago in Sioux Falls, South Dakota. He had lived in it for 30 years.

Dad gave me, after hooking up the electricity, a small lamp, telling me to "plug it in wherever you go." You can imagine the condition of the rest of the trailer! After Dad connected the fuel oil barrel to the furnace, I opened the door and lit the pilot light. Three months later I walked over to Dad's trailer across the road and told him I was going to have to move out of his trailer—the black soot was getting all over everything, even the cobwebs. Dad said, "well, what's the matter?" He came over and reached his hand to the top of the door and pulled a sliding door down and it fixed the problem. I noticed, when I came home from work that my breakfast dishes where green. There was no trap in the drain. I fixed everything, even putting a light in each room. After living in it for six months he told me that the only time he plugged in the hot water tank was when he needed hot water. There was blood all over the inside, from a nose bleed.

About the middle of the carpenter school, his friends called me in Rapid City, and told me Dad was dying from a nose bleed and that he had been drunk a week. I stayed in school. It was the last big drunk that he was ever on.

Dad had bought a new trailer just before I arrived in Casper. When he hooked up the water, he connected it to the natural gas line, damaging the furnace, hot water tank, and oven.

For my second job, the company bought me a pair of new hard-toed shoes. Dad said, "he never did get a pair in 30 years."

One of Dad's previous bosses noticed the same last name and told me he had to lay him off one time. He was acting a little funny on the job. He found a bottle in Dad's tool box. Another time I guess the boss was standing between him and his work, he said if you would get out of my road I could get some work done.

At the Alcove Dam he fell off the scaffold into the water, but he told his boss he went to sleep and to this day, the guy believes that.

He lived across the road in the trailer park and one day when I arrived home from work it was 30 to 40 below zero. He had the hood up on the truck and it wouldn't start. After a few attempts with either in the carburetor, he must have put the rest of the can in, and broke something in the engine. The sad part is, he never had any place to go.

Dad went to work in Gillette, Wyoming, on a school house that had just started. In about a week he was back. I accidentally ran into him at one of our favorite restaurants. He said "Mick, I saw some ducks flying south and that's where I'm headed."

Lake Andes, Ill. Construction Trailer park—hot and dry.

He asked me if I would buy his new trailer? Remembering the water caper, I decided not to.

He then sold the trailer that I was living in to a sheepherder, but his wife wouldn't live in it.

After buying a trailer for cash, he drove buy several times in his new truck, as I moved my stuff, with the Volks Wagon.

When I left Rapid City, Mom started to take drivers training and she got a drivers license, for the first time in her life.

The same day she got her drivers license, she bought a used Dodge and filled it with gas and drove it home. She parked it in a shed with an open door. At midnight the Dam on the Rapid City Creek was washed out and 237 people lost their lives with blocks of homes and other property destroyed—including the Dodge, which was the one and only car that Mom ever owned. She never drove a car again.

Dad sold his new trailer "as is." That meant TV, pots, pans, dish rags, towels, silverware, broom sheets, and pillow cases. He went to Miller, Missouri. That's a good place to leave him, since he was born in Joplin.

In Casper I attended a church that believed solely in one verse: **Acts 2 v 38** *Then Peter said unto them, Repent, and be baptized every one of you in the name of Jesus Christ for the remission of sins, and ye shall receive the gift of the Holy Ghost.* The church down the street wasn't much better.

For 15 years I had been seeking a mate, but in most churches it seemed as if the women were either 12 and under—or 60 and over. My son left to live in Texas after two years of college to be closer to his mother, who was living there.

What does the four Gospels, Revelation, and Psalms say about relationships?

Revelation 7 v 11 - 12 *And all the angels stood round about the throne, and about the elders and the four beasts, and fell before the throne on their faces, and worshiped God, Saying, Amen: Blessing, and glory, and wisdom, and thanksgiving, and honor, and power, and might, be unto our God for ever and ever. Amen.*

Revelation 4 v 8 *And the four beasts had each of them six wings about him; and they were full of eyes within: and they rest not day and night, saying, HOLY, HOLY, HOLY, Lord God almighty, which was, and is, and* *is to come.* **Psalm chapters 145 - 150** *Make reference to, " praise to God." 145 v 10 All thy works shall praise thee, O Lord; and thy saints shall bless thee. v 11 They shall speak of the glory of thy kingdom, and talk of thy power; v 20 The Lord preserveth all them that love him: but all the wicked will he destroy. 146 v 3 Put not your trust in princes, nor in the son of man, (any human being) in whom there is no help. 147 v 5 Great is our Lord, and of great power: his understanding is infinite.*

Psalm 148 *All creation to Praise the Lord. v 1 Praise ye the Lord:* (abbreviated) *heavens, heights, angels, hosts, sun and moon, stars of light, ye heavens of heavens, waters v 5 Let them praise the name of the LORD: for he commanded, and they were created. v 6 He hath also established them for ever and ever: he hath made a decree which shall not pass. from the earth, ye dragons, and all deeps, fire, and hail:*(we have a weather girl that can't say hail it comes out Hell) *snow, vapor, wind, mountains, hills, fruitful trees, cedars, beasts, cattle, creeping things, flying foul, kings of the earth, people, princes, judges of the earth, young men, maidens, old men, children,* (sounds like evolution to me) *149 v 4 For the Lord taketh pleasure in his people: he will beautify the meek with salvation. 150 v 3 Praise him with the sound of the trumpet, psaltery and harp, tumbrel and dance, stringed instruments, organs, loud cymbals, high-sounding cymbals,* (their is at least one denomination that has no music) Still on relationships So far we have read about the angels etc., toward God.

St Matthew 22 v 36 - 39 *Master, which is the great commandment in the law? Jesus said unto him, Thou shalt love the Lord thy God with all thy heart, and with all thy soul, and with all thy mind. This is the first and great commandment. And the second is like unto it, thou shalt love thy neighbor as thyself.* On these two commandments hang all the law and the prophets.

St John 5 v 42 & 43 (above) *But I know you, that ye have not the love of God in you. Those things that happened to me produced the love in my Heart, that only can come from God. Thou shalt* (will) *love thy neighbor as thyself.*

St Matthew 10 v 8 *Heal the sick, cleanse the leapers, raise the dead, cast out devils*: (you may have these powers) *freely ye have received, freely give*. This is what he means by loving your neighbor as yourself.

Would you invest $5000 in your neighbor not expecting any return? I did that. It was really much more than that because I used one of my best houses for two years writing a book. It was to reveal the truth, but no one wants to here the truth. Jesus had an advantage in the fact that he spoke in parables, much of the time. The book ended up in the garage.

Remember, God loves his Son, He gave Him the word to reveal to the world that we are to be judged by.

At Paul's conversion, where is the power that God has at His command?

The next time you see a Monarch butterfly go by, do me a favor and read Acts 9 v 3 - 5.

St Luke 14 v 26 *If any man come to me, and hate not his father, and mother, and wife, and children, and brethren, and sisters, yea, and his own life also, he cannot be my disciple*. Those of you that have found a life on this earth that you would die for, you are in trouble.

What would be the reason for you to seek God if you're already happy?

A professor that taught in their Bible college called his church a social affair. A carpenter friend of mine who did odd jobs said he went to church to get work. What is the reason that you go?

When my son left, I put an ad in the news paper for someone to date. It had been 15 years. One of the girls was okay. I bought a house for cash and we moved in together. I love my God with all, "thy heart and with all thy soul and with all thy mind."

Before you start throwing rocks, what about the Lord's Prayer above?

St Matthew 6 v 10 Thy kingdom come. Thy will be done in earth, as it is in heaven.

St Luke 20 v 35 *But they which shall be accounted worthy to obtain that world, and the resurrection from the dead, neither marry, nor are given in marriage:*

St Matthew 19 v 4 - 6 *And he answered and said unto them, Have ye not read, that he which made them at the beginning made them male and female, And said, For this cause shall a man leave father and mother, and shall cleave to his wife: and they twain shall be one flesh? Wherefore they are no more twain, but one flesh. What therefore God hath joined together, let not man put asunder.*

The problem is, God is not putting all the marriages together. Who would more likely stay together: "if they thought God had put them together" or the ones that had a performance in a church?

St Matthew 10 v 37, 39 *He that loveth father or mother more than me is not worthy of me: and he that loveth son or daughter more than me is not worthy of me. He that findeth his life shall lose it: and he that looseth his life for my sake shall find it. You don't have to yoke yourself up with, believers. It's best, but not necessary.*

St Matthew 24 v 40 - 41 *Then shall two be in the field; the one shall be taken, and the other left. v 41 Two women shall be grinding at the mill; the one shall be taken, and the other left.*

After working 13 years as a union carpenter, the work became scarce. I started going to college and lacked one semester of graduating. About the same time, I had started college, with the money I had saved, one at a time I bought houses or duplexes for CASH and fixed them up. Either I rented or sold them. At the peak of my endeavor I accumulated 13 units, and four cars with the deeds or titles in the bank vault. What sells is books that tell you to borrow money until your eyeballs drop out of your head. You're not even an American until you have a 30-year loan! I eventually started investing in the stock market, which was good, bad, and ugly.

A word of advice: the corporation I bought failed because I was weak financially. The rental business is like war, if you are weak, your chances are slim to none you will be successful. So go ahead and throw a chair through the wall—I can fix it. One time I thought the electricity had been turned off, they took all the light bulbs with them, but that is another book.

After the Rapid City flood in 1972, Dad did the rough carpenter work at $20.00 an hour.

Then I went from Casper, Wyoming to do the finish work. Mom hung on to a chest of drawers that probably saved her life. Ironically, Dad had made that chest of drawers.

Dad had hung the entry storm door. He ask me to come over to it, and there was about a two inch whole at the bottom. He said he, "didn't know what happened." I pushed the adjustable part down and covered up the hole.

One day they were going to go to the lumber yard and Dad had a flat tire. He put his spare tire on the passenger side before Mom got there. She was living in a house that she rented temporarily. She opened the door and couldn't get in the truck. Dad sitting there said, "well you have been getting in here." Then he remembered that he had left the jack under the axle. While working on the house he lived behind it in her garage. (Dirt floor.) After Mom sold her house to the government she came over to Casper and bought a house for cash in Casper, Wyoming.

Dad would visit us in Casper from time to time from Missouri. In 1981 I had bought a Holliday Rambler 32 ft. self-contained travel trailer for cash. It was equipped with everything one could ask for. He talked with Mom and me in the house a short time and said, let's go out and look at your trailer. He opened the door and followed me inside. I turned to explain something to him and all I saw was his back going out the door.

Eventually Mom was unable to take care of herself and we started hiring 24-hour care. It fit right in with me buying real estate. I could leave whatever I was doing at any time. We never had to have a real qualified person, so we definitely never got one. The duties included putting her leg brace on the polio leg and fix her breakfast, lunch, and supper. Then, after Mom watched TV to about ten, the duties included taking her brace off and putting her in bed. In the night you had to help get her up at least once, and set her on the portable potty. We went through a lot of help—they either quit or Mom fired them. We had one girl go after a package of cigarettes and never return. When there was any kind of problem, I would have to go over to her house and take over the regular duties if the girl left. Then we would put an add in the newspaper and hire another girl. I would have to live there until we got help.

Every Saturday was the girl's day off and it was my Job to give Mom a bath. We had a lift in the tub that was a great help. Because the brace had to be removed, she was taken to her bed in the wheel chair. The groceries were also bought on Saturday. But the bureaucracy was always a problem.

Mom read in the news paper that she could get help with her natural gas bill. I went down to sign up, they ask me about her income. When I told them Mom had full-time help, they added the two incomes together and we didn't qualify, since both were living in the same house.

Mickey and Paul.

Eventually Mom had to be put in a nursing home when she couldn't walk. She was there four years. Each month, I paid $2000 of a $3,000 bill of my money. I had to quit remodeling houses. Mom was born in 1911, she died on the eleventh day of the eleventh month in 1994.

Two days later I went over to the nursing home to get her things. The staff told me to go through the door "over there." I opened the door, which led outside, and found all her worldly possessions buried under snow.

Those of you that don't take care of your parents to the end will have to answer for it. No matter, "how they raised you." Dad never knew it, but I would have used all of my resources to help him until he died, if there was a problem. He passed away the same year, June 1994.

The house that I bought when mom went into the nursing home was the last. After she passed away I was able to do the extensive remodeling that it needed. With the thought, that I was going to live in it myself, the city inspectors let me do all or most of the work myself. Including the plumbing and most of the electrical.

They say if you want anything done right do it yourself. The original house it was as if it never was completed. With the abstract in hand, along with a history of natrona county I am sure the original builder was a deputy sheriff that came upon a boot leger that shot him with a twelve gage shoot gun.

It was a massive all brick structure with only one bed room and a murphy bed that dropped down out of the wall. At the time I bought it the murphy bed was laying out in the leaky garage so I dismantled it completly A man sand blasted it and painted the main bed gold with the other parts black.

Half of the attic was already livable so I decided to put a second story on it The stair way was the biggest problem. A circular one, it is hard to get anything up or down them. I used part of the formal dining room to make a normal stairway.

In a older neighborhood where it's located, to keep the cost down is a problem. The original house had two shingle roofs and one asphalt. I tore off all of it myself, and then replaced it with a wood shingles. At the time I bought all the shingles in Casper, Denver, and Rivertan, and waited for the second shipment from Canada.

On the inside I removed one of the two doors in the small kitchen so that I could put some new cabinets in. In the front room the ceiling was sagging, so I tore the lath and plaster off of the two by fours. Reading in the news paper, there was some two by fours the same as mine. I doubled up on them and put beams underneath to carry the second floor. On top of them I stained some outside plywood sheeting white and the two by fours and beams a dark stain, "early American."

My sister came from Wisconsin, brother from Tocoma, Washington, my son from Texas—they all liked the house. I don't get to see them as often as I would like, as most relatives now days are scattered to different states. I try to go visit them at least once a year. I helped move my brother to Oklahome, at the time we kept about a half day ahead of a storm. In the middle of Wyoming the bearings burn up on one of the wheels. We went the rest of the way with only one tire on one side of a fifth wheel trailer.

Most of my life I was the black sheep and none of the family thought I had a chance of being a success in life. As the scripture says, nothing is impossible for God.

When I got through with the house I used it to write a book, for two years. After it was edited I never recognized my own book. The editor sent two partial manuscrips off to publishers. They said they only published books from Mr. Billy Graham and Mr. Shuller. Three more years went by and I decided to try it again, remembering a verse in the Bible, I came across an advertisement in the *Veteran of Foreign Wars* magazine, of a possible publisher in Canada. **St John 4 v 44** *For Jesus himself testified, that a prophet hath no honor in his own country.*

On Noah's boat there were eight people, and according to Genesis, God destroyed all the rest of humanity. God said that He would not destroy man with water again, so He set in the sky a rainbow to remind Him of His covenant. **Genesis 6 v 5** *And God saw that the wickedness of man was great in the earth, and that every imagination of the thoughts of his heart was only evil continually.*

God knew that man would go in a circle and come to the exact same place as in the day of Noah. He recognized the fact that man needed a savior. Instead of destroying man as before with water, He would have His Son die on the cross for our sins. The requirement is that mankind has to believe in their heart on the works that Jesus did.

There might be another method for a different kind of person, but either one, you must be born again from above.

The scripture tells us that few will find the way. The question is then, what is that number? Keep in mind that only eight was saved in the flood in Noah's day. Has God ever changed his mind? **Genesis 6 v 6** *And it repented the lord that he had made man on the earth, and it grived him at his heart.*

 Do you want to look at the people in this world the way they are, or use welding goggles and blinders that Dad used to use to put on the work horses?

Twenty-seven words in Genesis 6 v 5 generally describes the world in which we live today.

The proof that there is not one bit of Bible, that one associates himself with, is the ruling of the law that child molesters must place a sign in front of where they live.

If a child molester is saved as I was, I can't imagine a child molester repeating the same crime again. I am thankful that I am a Child of God.

The so-called Christians have not said a word. In their silence it condemns them.

Most of the sermons are derived from the Old Testament—okay, if you want the Old Testament, let's do that.

LEVITICUS

Chapter 1 *And the Lord called unto Moses, and spake unto him out of the tabernacle of the congregation, saying, Speak unto the children of Israel, and say unto them, If any man of you bring an offering unto the lord, ye shall bring your offering unto the Lord, ye shall bring your offering of the cattle, even of the herd, and of the flock. If his offering be a burnt sacrifice of the herd, let him offer a male without blemish: he shall offer it of his own voluntary will at the door of the tabernacle of the congregation before the Lord. And he shall put his hand upon the head of the burnt offering. Etc.*

Mickey R. Mullen

The Way, The Truth, and The Life

ISBN 155212774-5